THE
TOP 100
OMEGA-3
RECIPES

D0048681

THE
TOP 100
OMEGA-3
RECIPES

**Penny Doyle and
Audrey Deane**

REDUCE YOUR RISK OF HEART DISEASE
KEEP YOUR BRAIN ACTIVE AND AGILE

DUNCAN BAIRD PUBLISHERS

LONDON

The Top 100 Omega-3 Recipes
Penny Doyle and Audrey Deane

Distributed in the USA and Canada by
Sterling Publishing Co., Inc.
387 Park Avenue South
New York, NY 10016-8810

This edition first published in the UK and USA in 2009 by
Duncan Baird Publishers Ltd
Sixth Floor, Castle House
75–76 Wells Street
London W1T 3QH

Managing Editor: Grace Cheetham
Editor: Katey Mackenzie
Managing Designer: Daniel Sturges
Designer: Sue Bush
Commissioned photography: Simon Scott
Food stylist: Mari Mererid Williams
Prop stylist: Helen Trent

Typeset in Helvetica Condensed
Color reproduction by Colourscan, Singapore
Printed in China by Imago

Library of Congress Cataloging-in-Publication Data available

ISBN: 978-1-84483-733-5
10 9 8 7 6 5 4 3 2 1

**Our thanks go to our wonderful families and
friends for their willingness to try our recipes
and for their honest feedback and sustained
support throughout the writing of this book.**

Publisher's note
**The information in this book is not intended as
a substitute for professional medical advice and
treatment. If you are pregnant or breastfeeding or
have any special dietary requirements or medical
conditions, it is recommended that you consult a
medical professional before following any of the
information or recipes contained in this book. Duncan
Baird Publishers, or any other persons who have
been involved in working on this publication, cannot
accept responsibility for any errors or omissions,
inadvertent or not, that may be found in the recipes or
text, nor for any problems that may arise as a result
of preparing one of these recipes or following the
advice contained in this work.**

Notes on the Recipes
All ingredients are fresh unless otherwise stated
Use fresh fish. When preparing fresh fish, wash it briefly
under cold running water before use
Use large eggs and medium fruit and vegetables
1 tsp = 5ml   1 tbsp = 15ml   1 cup = 240ml

Symbols are used to identify even small amounts of an
ingredient. Dairy food may include cow, goat or sheep milk.
The vegetarian symbol is given to recipes using cheese; check
the manufacturer's label before purchase to ensure cheeses are
vegetarian. Ensure that only the relevantly identified foods are
given to anyone with a food allergy or intolerance.

For information about custom editions, special sales,
premium and corporate purchases, please contact
Sterling Special Sales Department at 800-805-5489
or specialsales@sterlingpub.com.

contents

KEY TO SYMBOLS

Contains Fish Omega-3: Long-chain omega-3 from fish sources can be used immediately by our bodies. It is therefore the most useful to us.

Contains Vegetarian Omega-3: Short-chain omega-3 comes from plant sources such as oils, flax seed, soy, and hemp products and is an invaluable source of omega-3 for vegetarians.

Vegetarian: Recipes with this symbol contain no meat, fish, or poultry. Vegetarian recipes can be a good choice for those suffering from digestive problems. Check labels carefully to ensure that cheeses are suitable for vegetarians.

Contains Dairy: These recipes use milk, butter, cheese, or ingredients containing dairy, such as yogurt or pesto.

Contains Egg: These recipes use egg or products containing egg, such as mayonnaise or egg noodles.

Contains Gluten: Gluten is a protein found in wheat, rye, barley, and oats. It causes no problems for most people. These recipes are not suitable for coeliacs.

Contains Nuts: These dishes include one or more types of nuts so are best avoided if you have a nut allergy.

Contains Seeds: These recipes are unsuitable for those who have been advised to avoid seeds and seed oils.

Contains Wheat: Wheat is found in many foods, including flour, couscous, cereals, and pasta. Avoid these recipes if you are intolerant or allergic to wheat.

INTRODUCTION

We are bombarded daily with claims about the amazing ability of fish oils to prevent heart attacks, reduce the pain of rheumatoid arthritis, lower bad cholesterol, increase good cholesterol, and make our children more intelligent. But how much of this is true, and how much is simply just good press? You may be pleasantly surprised about how far-reaching some of the scientifically proven benefits of omega-3 can be. In some cases, research is ongoing and dynamic, but the hard fact remains that everyone can benefit from including a range of omega-3 fats in their daily diet. Indeed, so strong is the clinical evidence that many governments allow food manufacturers to make health claims about omega-3 on their products.

The great news is that increasing your intake is easy using this book, whether you've been given specific advice to increase your intake of omega-3 fats or are simply trying to eat more as part of a healthy balanced diet. Although the best source of omega-3 is oily fish, such as salmon and mackerel, many people struggle to eat enough. Fortunately, many other foods contain omega-3 as well. The recipes in this book show you how to cook food that will contribute significantly to your weekly intake, providing inspiration and confidence to prepare foods containing fish, plus innovative ideas for including non-fish omega-3 sources, such as tofu and flax seed. You'll find one hundred delicious recipes that can be prepared and eaten throughout the day, each accompanied by a breakdown of the nutritional facts per portion. They have family living in mind, are uncomplicated and, crucially, can be prepared using readily available ingredients.

HOW MUCH OMEGA-3 DO WE NEED EACH DAY?

Omega-3 fats are found in both fish and vegetarian sources, so it's easy to include them in your food and still eat a varied diet. The recommended daily guidelines do vary globally, which can make it difficult to decide how much you should eat. However, all organizations agree that we typically do not eat enough and that anything we can do to increase our intake is a good thing. Taking all of these recommendations into account, you should aim to eat up to 1g of fish omega-3 per day. The nutrition facts provided with each of this book's recipes will help you see how to reach this amount.

There are no specific recommendations for vegetarian omega-3, so these can be included whenever you can.

Good for your heart

Heart disease has been described by the World Health Organization (WHO) as a true pandemic that respects no borders. Hereditary factors do come into play, but lifestyle factors are also important, including exercise, stress, and diet. Increasing your intake of omega-3, fiber, fruit, and vegetables, while reducing saturated fats, can help. Fish omega-3 in the diet is especially beneficial for those who have suffered a heart attack because it might reduce the risk of further attacks. Omega-3 is thought to work by:

- Lowering bad blood cholesterol and other fats, while simultaneously raising good cholesterol levels.
- Reducing the clogging up of coronary arteries.

- Encouraging a regular heart rhythm.
- Reducing blood pressure.

Japanese people who eat a lot of vegetarian omega-3, such as from canola oil and soy, have been shown to have longer life expectancies, and those who have already suffered one heart attack have half the chance of suffering a further attack. More research is needed, but these are certainly encouraging results for vegetarians.

Good for your brain

Oily fish is traditionally known as good brain food. Indeed, omega-3 fats make up eight percent of the human brain. Fish omega-3 is vital to brain and eye function. It is passed from mother to baby in the last stages of pregnancy and then after birth through breast milk. Consequently, many infant formulas are now supplemented with omega-3.

Omega-3 fats have also been linked to helping to reduce depression. In various studies, large doses of omega-3 fats have been seen to reduce symptoms of depression. There are also proven links between low omega-3 levels and post-natal depression. It is thought that much of this may be due to the fact that the mother may transfer much of her stores of omega-3 to the unborn baby, thus leaving her own body depleted. This situation can become even worse with further pregnancies if the mother fails to replenish her omega-3 levels between babies.

It's not just mothers' and babies' brains that benefit from a regular source of omega-3 fats, however. A large population study in the Netherlands identified fish consumption as a potential protective factor against both dementia and Alzheimer's disease. This is a promising area for research, and it may well be that the worldwide food agencies will need to revise their omega-3 guidelines specifically for the elderly in light of this emerging evidence.

Good for children's behavior

There is solid evidence that omega-3 fats can help to improve symptoms of behavioral disturbances in children, including Attention Deficit Hyperactivity Disorder (ADHD). Improvements have also been seen in studies where young offenders took omega-3 supplements. Some scientists believe that adolescent behavioral problems may result from a depletion of omega-3 levels due to the brain's massive developmental spurt during puberty.

Strokes

Heart disease and stroke are the first and third most common killers in America, with the two issues often co-existing. A stroke is similar to a heart attack in the brain, and brain cells may die, seriously affecting speech, movement, and memory. Because of the association of heart attacks and stroke (also known under the umbrella term cardiovascular disease), fish oils are routinely recommended to stroke sufferers to help prevent further strokes and heart attacks. The ways that fish oils may work to prevent further strokes are similar to those for the heart: reducing blood clots and, possibly, blood pressure. Omega-3 supplements are not routinely recommended to stroke sufferers taking warfarin as medication, however, since when combined with the drug they can make the blood too thin.

Diabetes

There are an estimated 20 million diabetics in the United States. Sufferers are at particular risk of heart disease and, for this reason alone, eating more omega-3 as part of a balanced diabetic diet is good advice.

There is also evidence indicating that omega-3 may make insulin work better and help with the management of the disease by either reducing the amount of insulin injections needed or even delaying the onset of type I diabetes in children.

Rheumatoid Arthritis and other Inflammatory Diseases

Fish omega-3 fats help to bolster the body's natural immunity and reduce the production of chemicals associated with the unnecessary and painful inflammatory responses seen in rheumatoid arthritis, childhood asthma, cystic fibrosis, and Crohn's disease. For rheumatoid arthritis sufferers particularly, there is good evidence to show that taking very high doses of omega-3 (up to 10 times that recommended for the average person) may help to reduce stiffness, tenderness, and pain and could even reduce the body's dependence upon steroid drugs—

great news for those who have suffered their various unpleasant side effects. Meeting these high doses of omega-3 would almost certainly require fish-oil supplements, but a diet rich in omega-3 fats would make a valuable dietary contribution nevertheless.

Cancer

In animal experiments, omega-3 fats have been shown to limit the spread of cancer to other parts of the body, particularly from the prostate. It is thought that omega-3 fats may help boost the body's immunity and block the action of the fats that act as an energy source to the cancer cells. Though current scientific thinking is that omega-3 may not prevent cancer, the World Cancer Research Fund nevertheless recommends that oily fish should be included in our daily diets in light of known wider benefits and with the hope that it may offer some protection from the disease.

WHICH INGREDIENTS CONTAIN OMEGA-3?

The best-known source of omega-3 is oily fish, such as salmon and mackerel, but as you can see from the table below, there is a very wide range of sources. These include other fish and seafood, listed on the left of the table, and vegetarian sources, listed on the right. The table gives the amount of omega-3 fats per portion.

Fish Omega-3	Average Portion Size	Amount Omega-3 Per Portion	Vegetarian Omega-3	Average Portion Size	Amount Omega-3 Per Portion
Anchovy (fresh, in oil, and canned)	8 fillets/2oz.	1.0g	Arugula	5oz.	0.2g
			Black beans (dried)	½ cup	0.2g
Anchovy paste	2oz.	1.0g	Canola oil	1 tbsp.	1.40g
Cod	5½oz.	0.4g	Flaxseed	1 tbsp.	3.42g
Crab (including brown meat)	9oz.	2.0g	Flaxseed oil	1 tbsp.	8.0g
			Hemp seed	5 tbsp.	2.0g
Haddock	5½oz.	0.3g	Hemp seed oil	1 tbsp.	2.87g
Halibut	5½oz.	0.5g	Kale	1 cup	0.1g
Herring	5½oz.	2.5g	Pinto beans	⅓ cup	0.1g
Mackerel	7oz.	4.6g	Red kidney beans (canned)	½ cup	0.3g
Mackerel fillet (smoked)	3½oz./fillet	2.3g			
Mussels	5½oz.	0.7g	Soybeans (cooked)	1 cup	0.6g
Pollock	5½oz.	0.6g	Soybeans (dried)	¼ cup	0.5g
Shrimp	3½oz.	0.5g	Soy flour	1oz.	0.4g
Rollmop (herring)	2½oz.	0.9g	Soy oil	1 tbsp.	1.1g
Salmon (smoked)	1oz./slice	0.6g	Soy milk	7fl. oz.	0.4g
Salmon steak	4½oz.	2.0g	Spinach	2¼oz.	0.1g
Sardine (fresh and canned)	4½oz.	1.9g	Tofu	3½oz.	0.6g
			Walnuts	1¾oz.	4.54g
Scallops	3½oz.	0.2g	Walnut oil	1 tbsp.	1.56g
Sea bass fillet	5½oz.	0.9g			
Squid	5½oz.	0.7g			
Trout	5½oz.	1.4g			
Trout (smoked)	5½oz.	2.0g			
Tuna (canned)	3½oz.	0.6g			
Tuna steak (fresh)	4½oz./steak	1.5g	Data source: USDA, Fineli, HMSO		

OMEGA-3 INGREDIENTS

The recipes in this book use foods that are naturally high in omega-3 fats rather than those that are fortified. A growing number of fortified foods are now on sale, including milk, dairy spreads, eggs, baked beans, and orange juice; but since their omega-3 levels vary and they are not widely available, they have not been included. They can boost omega-3 intake, but can be expensive, may be low in omega-3, and are often unsuitable for vegetarians.

Buying, preparing, and storing fresh fish and seafood

Prepared fish is easily available, and a good fishmonger will be more than happy to gut or fillet fish. The following tips will help you buy the best fish and seafood:

- For whole fish, always look for bright eyes, a clean smell, and bright red gills.
- For fillets and steaks, look for firm, clean flesh without a fishy smell.
- For shellfish, look for shells that are closed, or that close when touched, and that feel full, not light.
- Always buy fish as fresh as possible, ideally the same day you plan to cook it.

Storage of fresh fish is very important and it should be chilled or frozen immediately after purchase. Fish for freezing should be well wrapped and stored for no longer than two months. Frozen fish should be defrosted in a fridge overnight.

Canned fish and seafood

Canned fish and seafood are very useful when fresh versions are unavailable, and generally have as much omega-3 as fresh. The exception is tuna: the canning process removes much of the omega-3. Be aware that canned crab is often just the white meat (often labeled "lump meat"), which is not a good omega-3 source. Look for the brown meat, often sold as "dressed" crab.

Tofu

Tofu, also known as "bean curd," is a low-fat protein- and calcium-rich vegetarian food made from soybeans. Of the two main types, firm and silken, only firm tofu is a reasonable source of vegetarian omega-3. Both types of tofu are available in supermarkets and health-food stores.

Soybeans and Legumes

Soybeans are the best source of vegetarian omega-3 of all the legumes. Though dried soybeans do take some time to cook after soaking (about 2 hours), this time can be halved by use of a pressure cooker, and canned soybeans are also available. Green soybeans (edamame beans) are also now available, but these young beans are not a good omega-3 source.

Oils

Canola, flax seed, hemp seed, and walnut oils are all widely available in large supermarkets and health-food stores. Some, particularly hemp and walnut oil, can enhance cooking with their wonderfully nutty flavors. Flax seed and hemp seed oils need to be kept in the refrigerator to slow the breakdown of their essential fats. Don't try to fry with them, however, as they smoke at high temperatures.

Seeds and Nuts

Keep a variety of seeds in the kitchen cupboard to add texture, flavor, and essential nutrients to your food. The ones that we have used widely in our recipes, such as flax seed and hemp, are richest in omega-3 fats. Since whole seeds tend to pass through the digestive system untouched, they need to be cracked or ground to allow their nutrients to be released. Most commercially available flax seed and hemp seed is already cracked; alternatively, you can toast and crush seeds using a mortar and pestle or a blender.

IF I EAT MORE FISH, WILL I EXPOSE MYSELF TO CONTAMINANTS?

Concerns about toxins in oily fish are important. However, we know that the benefits of oily fish do outweigh the potential disadvantages. Larger fish, such as shark, marlin, swordfish, and tuna are of more concern, and worldwide food agencies advise that pregnant or breastfeeding women should limit their intake of all oily fish.

WHAT ABOUT SUSTAINABILITY?

It would be wrong to write this book without considering sustainability of fish stocks—a growing global issue. According to the Marine Conservation Society (MCS), seventy percent of the world's fish stocks are now fully fished, over-fished, or depleted. Most of the endangered species, such as cod, are not oily, and the thorny issue of sustainability is now being addressed by governments through the use of fish quotas and by campaigners who are increasing consumer awareness.

Global organizations such as the Marine Stewardship Council (MSC) are at work to improve the environmental standards of fisheries to ensure sustainability. The key is clearly to eat fish sustainably caught in a way that minimizes environmental damage. Fish farming is big business, and about one third of seafood eaten world-wide is farmed. You would be forgiven for thinking that fish farming would be the answer to sustainability issues, but there remain environmental concerns, particularly about the recent surge of salmon farming. The MSC checks all of these aspects, and those that pass receive the MSC "blue check" of endorsement, which we should all be looking for. Organic fish is generally farmed or fished with emphasis on welfare and sustainability. Visit the MSC website at www.msc.org for more information about your local suppliers.

UNSATURATED FATS

Monounsaturated	Polyunsaturated	
Omega-**9**	Omega-**3**	Omega-**6**
Olive oil	Fish oil	Sunflower oil
Avocado oil	Canola oil	Sesame oil
	Soy oil	Peanut oil
	Flax seed oil	Corn oil

KEY FACTS ABOUT FATS

Fat in our food is divided into three types: saturated, monounsaturated, and polyunsaturated. Saturated fats are mainly from meat, butter, and lard, whereas monounsaturated and polyunsaturated fats are mainly from vegetables and fish. These fats are further split into groups: omega-3, 6, and 9.

Unlike omega-9 fats, which our bodies can produce themselves, as well as get from food, we rely solely on food for omega-3 and omega-6 fats. They are often referred to as "essential fats." The reason so much emphasis is placed on omega-3, and not omega-6 fats, is that we eat plenty of omega-6 fats: modern diets are naturally high in sunflower oil and corn oils from processed foods but not in omega-3. Indeed, over-consumption of omega-6 fats hinders the body's ability to use omega-3 efficiently.

Getting the balance right

It is estimated that we eat between 10 and 20 times more omega-6 than omega-3 fats. Eating too many omega-6 fats reduces the benefits of the omega-3 fats that we eat. A sensible ratio is around four times as much omega-6 as omega-3.

Why is there so much emphasis on omega-3 fats from fish?

The reason is that omega-3 fats from fish are the most useful to us. Omega-3 in oily fish is structurally different from the omega-3 found in vegetarian sources. Omega-3 fats in oily fish are predominantly "long chain," whereas omega-3 fats from vegetarian sources are all "short chain." The full names of the long-chain fats are Eicosapentanoic Acid (EPA) and Docosahexanoic Acid (DHA), while short-chain fats are Alpha Linolenic Acid (ALA). Our bodies can convert small amounts of short-chain fats into long-chain fats, but we are not very good at it, and it is slowed down by lifestyle factors, including diet and stress. That said, short-chain omega-3 has a useful role in boosting omega-3 intake and is the only source for non-fish eaters. The body then transforms long-chain EPA and DHA into prostaglandins— hormone-like compounds that play a role in regulating bodily functions, such as inflammation, blood clotting, sodium and potassium balance, and blood pressure.

The following general dietary advice will help you boost your omega-3 intake.

- Concentrate on eating fish sources of omega-3 but also include some vegetarian sources in your diet.
- Use canola oil in general cooking.
- Use organic milk, which contains about twice as much omega-3 as non-organic milk, or use omega-3 fortified milk.
- Substitute butter and dairy spreads with an omega-3 fortified product or

olive oil-based spreads, which are lower in omega-6 fats.

- Consider using soy products, such as milk, flour, spread, yogurts, and tofu, which contain some omega-3 fat and have other health benefits.

WHAT ABOUT OMEGA-3 SUPPLEMENTS?

There is a growing market for omega-3 supplements—the range is improving and, increasingly, they are made using sustainable fish sources. Supplements have an important role for those who need to eat higher than average amounts of omega-3 for therapeutic purposes, such as rheumatoid arthritis sufferers, who would not be able to achieve recommended intakes by diet alone.

Things to be aware of when buying omega-3 supplements:

- Make sure that the suggested daily dose will usefully contribute to boosting your omega-3 intake.

- Warfarin users should always seek medical advice if planning to take omega-3 supplements because warfarin may react negatively with omega-3 supplements, making blood too thin.

- Some vitamins, particularly vitamin A, can be toxic in large quantities and are often included in both multivitamin supplements and omega-3 capsules. Read the boxes carefully to make sure you are not "mega-dosing" on vitamins or minerals.

- Those suffering from angina, but who haven't had a heart attack, are not recommended to take fish-oil supplements because of studies suggesting negative effects. Boosting omega-3 intake using diet, however, is considered to be safe for these people.

Always seek professional help from a doctor or dietitian if you are unsure when taking nutritional supplements.

NUTRITION FACTS—MAKING THEM WORK FOR YOU

Every recipe in this book is accompanied by a nutritional analysis of one portion. An understanding of the nutritional values of each serving can help you reach your optimum omega-3 intake. The nutrient breakdown also lists the calories, fat, and saturated fat the recipe would contribute to your diet.

NUTRIENT	HOW DOES IT APPLY TO ME?
Energy (Kcal)	You must take into account the whole of your diet when counting calories. If you are trying to lose weight, make sure you eat the higher-calorie recipes with plenty of vegetables, salads, and starchy foods, such as potatoes, pasta, or rice, which have half the calories, weight for weight, as fatty foods.
Fat (g)	You can lower the fat and calorie content of the recipes by using lower-fat alternatives, such as milk, crème fraîche, and low-fat olive spreads, though these may not be suitable for the very young or old. Though by their nature omega-3-rich foods are not low in fat, within the context of a balanced diet, their benefits easily counteract this.
Saturated Fat (g)	We should all aim to eat fewer saturated fats to help keep our blood cholesterol low and improve overall health. For an adult woman, this equates to no more than about half of her total daily fat intake.
Vegetarian Omega-3 (g)	Vegetarian (short-chain) omega-3 is useful for those whose intake of oily fish is low. The more you eat, the better.
Fish Omega-3 (g)	Generally, the more fish (long-chain) omega-3 you eat, the better—although you need to remember the upper limits on intake because of concerns about toxicity. As a guide, an intake of up to 1g per day is considered safe.

BREAKFASTS

Kick-start your day with one of these delicious, healthy omega-3 breakfasts to fuel your body and your brain. Widely acknowledged as the most important meal of the day, breakfast is a chance to charge your body with energy and omega-3. Fruity Maple Oatmeal will leave you feeling full right through until lunch, and its secret ingredient—ground flax seed—is a rich source of omega-3. Breakfast Granola, with its crunchy, honeyed omega-3 nuts and seeds, tastes just as good as it looks. Tuna & Bacon Hash Browns make a filling power brunch for busy weekends, while on-the-go options like Oaty Breakfast Bars or Oaty Fruit Muffins mean there's no excuse for you to skip breakfast on even the most manic Monday.

breakfast granola

This is a great way to start the day because it's packed with energy and flavor. The oats and fruit will keep you feeling full all morning.

1 cup rolled oats
1 cup rolled jumbo oats
¼ cup whole flax seed
²/₃ cup crushed walnuts

¼ cup flax seed oil
¼ cup clear honey
½ cup raisins
½ cup dried cranberries

1 Preheat the oven to 275°F. Mix the oats, seeds, nuts, oil, and honey together in a bowl and stir until well coated.
2 Spread the mixture out onto two nonstick baking sheets to a depth of ½in. Bake 50 minutes or until golden brown. Remove from the oven and let cool 5 minutes.
3 Using a spatula, lightly break the mix into chunks. Let cool completely, then pour into a large bowl. Add the dried fruit and mix carefully, taking care not to break up the chunks, then serve.

SERVES 10

PREPARATION + COOKING
10 + 50 minutes

STORAGE
Store in an airtight container for up to 3 weeks.

SERVE THIS WITH...
plain yogurt
raspberries
blackberries

OMEGA-3 SOURCES
Whole flax seed, flax seed oil, walnuts

NUTRITIONAL FACTS PER PORTION
2.8g. vegetarian omega-3
277 calories
14g. fat
1.4g. saturated fat

Ⓥ ● ● ● ● ●

oaty breakfast bar

These nutritous breakfast bars are packed with delicious goodies. The energy from the oats will release slowly, staving off hunger pangs.

1 tbsp. canola oil
½ cup olive oil spread
¼ cup unrefined sugar
2 tbsp. light corn syrup
2 tbsp. maple syrup
1 cup rolled oats

4 cups puffed rice
¼ cup ground flax seed
scant ½ cup walnut pieces
scant ½ cup dried cranberries
scant ½ cup yogurt-covered
   raisins

1 Preheat the oven to 350°F. Grease a deep, nonstick 9in. baking pan with the oil.

2 Melt the olive oil spread in a pan, then stir in the sugar and corn syrup. Let cool, then add the maple syrup.

3 Mix the oats, puffed rice, flax seed, walnuts, and cranberries together. Stir in the syrup mixture, then add the yogurt-covered raisins and stir well.

4 Spoon onto the baking pan and spread to a depth of 1¼in. Press the mixture down with the back of a spoon and bake 20 minutes until golden.

5 Remove from oven and cut into 12 bars in the pan. Run a palette knife around the edges so that the bars don't stick. Remove from the pan after 10 minutes. Serve cold.

MAKES 12

PREPARATION + COOKING
10 + 20 minutes

STORAGE
Store on wax paper in an airtight container for up to 2 weeks.

SERVE THIS WITH...
dried apricots
dried cherries

OMEGA-3 SOURCES
Ground flax seed, walnuts, canola oil

NUTRITIONAL FACTS PER PORTION
1.7g. vegetarian omega-3
250 calories
13g. fat
1.6g. saturated fat

mango & banana smoothie

Smoothies have been gaining in popularity as a way of boosting fruit and vegetable intake. By making your own, you can use really fresh fruit to ensure that the vitamin content is as high as possible.

SERVES 1

PREPARATION
5 minutes

STORAGE
Do not refrigerate. Freeze for up to 1 month.

SERVE THIS WITH...
Fruity Maple Oatmeal (see page 25)

OMEGA-3 SOURCES
Flax seed oil

NUTRITIONAL FACTS PER PORTION
5g. vegetarian omega-3
438 calories
9g. fat
0.8g. saturated fat

2 tsp. flax seed oil
1 banana, peeled

½ mango, peeled, pitted, and chopped
1¼ cups orange juice

1 Put the flax seed oil, banana, mango, and orange juice in a blender or food processor and whizz until smooth.
2 Serve immediately or freeze into ice pop molds for the kids.

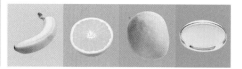

Ⓥ 🌐 🥄 🍃 🍶

fruity maple oatmeal

Ground flax seed is a quick and easy way to get omega-3 into your diet. Here it is added to oatmeal with a fruity twist.

2 cups rolled oats
3½ cups milk
2 dried apricots, chopped
3 tbsp. ground flax seed
¼ cup maple syrup

1 Mix the oats and milk together and heat gently in a large saucepan over low heat, stirring constantly. Cook 4 minutes, until the oats absorb the milk.
2 Stir in the apricots and cook another minute.
3 Stir in the ground flax seed and half the maple syrup. Serve immediately, drizzled with the remaining syrup.

SERVES 4

PREPARATION + COOKING
2 + 5 minutes

STORAGE
This is not suitable for the refrigerator or freezer.

SERVE THIS WITH...
Mango & Banana Smoothie
(see page 24)

OMEGA-3 SOURCES
ground flax seed

NUTRITIONAL FACTS PER PORTION
2.3g. vegetarian omega-3
400 calories
11g. fat
2.6g. saturated fat

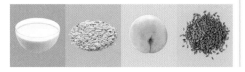

*american pancakes

OMEGA-3 SOURCES
Ground flax seed, canola oil

NUTRITIONAL FACTS PER PORTION
1.8g. vegetarian omega-3
278 calories
10g. fat
2g. saturated fat

Turbo-boost your system with these hearty healthy breakfast pancakes. Made with ground flax seed and cooked in canola oil, these little pancakes give you an omega-3 head start. They're surprisingly filling and will stave off hunger pangs until lunch.

1 cup self-rising flour
¼ cup ground flax seed
pinch of salt
¼ cup unrefined sugar

2 eggs
1 tsp. vanilla extract
1 cup milk
1 tbsp. canola oil

SERVES 4

PREPARATION + COOKING
15 + 10 minutes

STORAGE
Store the pancake batter
in a sealed container in the
refrigerator for up to 3 days.
Freeze for up to 1 month.

SERVE THIS WITH...
sliced banana
maple syrup

1 Sift the flour, ground flax seed, and salt into a mixing
bowl, tipping the bran from the ground flax seed in, too.
Add the sugar and make a well in the center.

2 Whisk the eggs in a small mixing bowl, add the vanilla
extract and milk and mix well. Gradually pour the egg
mixture into the dry ingredients, whisking as you pour
to form a smooth batter. Let rest 10 minutes.

3 Gently heat half the oil in a frying pan. Drop a large
tablespoon of the mixture into the pan—it will spread
out to about 4in. Cook the pancakes 3 or 4 at a time
3 minutes on the first side, then flip them over and cook
another 2 minutes. Serve immediately.

**You could make a
dairy-free version of
this recipe by using
soy milk instead of
regular milk.**

french toast

Perfect for chilly mornings, this classic breakfast is enduringly popular. Made with Omega Bread, it is packed with goodness.

2 eggs	**4 slices of Omega Bread**
¹⁄₃ cup milk	**(see page 72)**
	1 tbsp. canola oil

1 Beat the eggs and milk together in a bowl. Pour half the egg mixture into a shallow bowl and soak a slice of bread in it 10 seconds. Turn the bread over to soak another 10 seconds.

2 Heat the oil in a frying pan and fry the soaked bread 1 minute on each side or until golden.

3 Repeat with the other slices of bread, using the rest of the egg mix as required. Serve hot.

SERVES 4

PREPARATION + COOKING
5 + 10 minutes

STORAGE
This is not suitable for the refrigerator or freezer.

SERVE THIS WITH…
baked beans
bacon
freshly squeezed orange juice

OMEGA-3 SOURCES
Ground flax seed, flax seed, walnuts, hemp oil, canola oil

NUTRITIONAL FACTS PER PORTION
3.5g. vegetarian omega-3
325 calories
19g. fat
2.5g. saturated fat

Ⓥ ⓐ Ⓞ Ⓞ Ⓞ Ⓞ Ⓞ Ⓞ

oaty fruit muffins

Made in advance, these are an ideal on-the-go option for days when time is tight.

1 cup rolled oats
1¼ cups milk
⅔ cup walnuts
½ cup hemp oil
¾ cup unrefined sugar
1 egg

⅔ cup raisins
1¼ cups all-purpose flour, sifted
4 tsp. baking powder
1 tsp. salt

1 Preheat the oven to 400°F. Place 12 paper baking cups in a muffin pan.
2 Soak the oats in the milk 15 minutes. Toast the walnuts under the broiler 2 to 3 minutes, then put them in a plastic bag and bash them into pieces, using a rolling pin.
3 Beat together the oil, scant ⅔ cup of the sugar, and the egg. Add the raisins and walnuts and pour into the oat mix.
4 Beat in the flour, baking powder, and salt until smooth.
5 Divide between the muffin cups, sprinkle the rest of the sugar on top, and bake 20 to 25 minutes until golden.

MAKES 12

PREPARATION + COOKING
15 + 25 minutes

STORAGE
Store in an airtight container for 1 week. Freeze for up to 1 month.

SERVE THIS WITH...
Greek yogurt

OMEGA-3 SOURCES
Walnuts, hemp oil

NUTRITIONAL FACTS PER PORTION
2.5g. vegetarian omega-3
310 calories
17g. fat
2.3g. saturated fat

800

scrambled tofu on toast

This simple brunch dish is a refreshing alternative to an old favorite—scrambled eggs.

SERVES 4

PREPARATION + COOKING
20 minutes + 1 minute

STORAGE
Scrambled tofu can be stored in the refrigerator for 3 days. It is not suitable for freezing.

SERVE THIS WITH...
Mango & Banana Smoothie (see page 24)

OMEGA-3 SOURCES
tofu, hemp oil

NUTRITIONAL FACTS PER PORTION
2.5g. vegetarian omega-3
420 calories
24g. fat
3.9g. saturated fat

1oz. dried porcini mushrooms
1lb. 2oz. firm tofu, roughly cubed
2 tbsp. hemp oil
8 slices of wholewheat bread
olive oil spread, for spreading
2 tbsp. chopped parsley
salt
freshly ground black pepper

1 Soak the mushrooms in ¾ cup warm water 5 minutes.

2 Lightly mash the tofu into the mushroom mixture, using the back of a fork. Add the hemp oil and season with salt and pepper. Let marinate 15 minutes.

3 Gently warm the tofu mixture in a pan 1 minute.

4 Toast the bread and spread it with the olive oil spread.

5 Stir the parsley into the scrambled tofu and serve piled on the hot toast.

kedgeree

Traditionally made with smoked haddock, kedgeree also works well with smoked herring.

4 eggs
¼ cup frozen peas
2½ cups long grain rice, rinsed

9oz. canned smoked herring fillet, drained and skin removed
2 tsp. curry paste
¼ cup mayonnaise

1 Boil the eggs 10 minutes, then drain and drop into a bowl of cold water to cool completely. Meanwhile, boil the peas 5 minutes until tender. Drain and set aside.
2 While the eggs and peas are boiling, place the rice in a large pot of boiling water and boil 10 to 12 minutes until cooked. Drain, spoon into a serving dish, and separate the grains. Flake the smoked herring into the rice.
3 Mix the curry paste with the mayonnaise, then stir it into the rice, taking care not to break up the fish flakes.
4 Peel and coarsely chop the eggs. Mix the egg and peas into the rice and serve immediately.

SERVES 4

PREPARATION + COOKING
10 + 15 minutes

STORAGE
This is not suitable for the refrigerator or freezer.

SERVE THIS WITH...
broiled tomatoes
lemon wedges

OMEGA-3 SOURCES
smoked herring

NUTRITIONAL FACTS PER PORTION
1.5g. fish omega-3
682 calories
30g. fat
4.5g. saturated fat

OMEGA-3 SOURCES
Canola oil, salmon

NUTRITIONAL FACTS PER PORTION
1.2g. fish omega-3
0.7g. vegetarian omega-3
300 calories
22g. fat
4.3g. saturated fat

*smoked salmon omelet

Salmon packs a powerful punch when it comes to boosting your omega-3 intake. And it seems that the old adage is true—fish is good for your brain. Omega-3 fats are thought to aid a healthy, happy brain and may reduce the risk of Alzheimer's disease and dementia.

2 tbsp. canola oil
8 eggs, lightly beaten
4oz. mushrooms, finely sliced
2 tbsp. chopped chives

7oz. smoked salmon, sliced
  into ribbons
salt
freshly ground black pepper

SERVES 4

PREPARATION + COOKING
5 + 15 minutes

STORAGE
This can be kept in the refrigerator overnight, but is not suitable for freezing.

SERVE THIS WITH…
baked beans
broiled tomatoes
broiled portobello mushrooms

1 Heat half the oil in a small frying pan. Season the eggs with salt and pepper, then add half of them to the pan. Stir gently 2 minutes until the eggs begin to set. Using a wooden spoon, draw the edges toward the center, allowing the raw egg to run into the spaces.

2 Sprinkle half the mushrooms and half the chives over the omelet. Turn the heat down to low and cook about 5 minutes until the egg is firm. Transfer the omelet to a plate and keep warm.

3 Repeat steps 1 and 2 to make a second omelet.

4 Cut the omelets in half and lay the strips of salmon on top. Serve immediately.

Boost your omega-3 intake further by making this omelet using omega-3 enriched eggs.

smoked trout & poached egg on toast

Smoked trout has a more subtle flavor than smoked salmon but is equally delicious. This simple but indulgent start to the day will keep you going until lunch, topped up with a few pieces of fruit along the way.

1 tbsp. vinegar	7oz. smoked trout, sliced
4 eggs	salt
4 thick slices of bread	freshly ground black pepper
¼ cup butter	

1 Bring a pot of water to a boil, then add the vinegar and reduce the heat to a very low simmer.

2 Crack the eggs, one at a time, into the water. Bring back to a boil, remove from the heat, and let stand 3 minutes.

3 Meanwhile, toast the bread and spread it with the butter.

4 Using a slotted spoon, lift each egg out of the water. Let them drain a few seconds, then place them on the toast. Lay the smoked trout slices across the top, season with salt and black pepper, and serve.

SERVES 4

PREPARATION + COOKING
5 minutes + 5 minutes

STORAGE
This is not suitable for the refrigerator or freezer.

SERVE THIS WITH...
a toasted, buttered bagel instead of toast

OMEGA-3 SOURCES
Trout

NUTRITIONAL FACTS PER PORTION
0.5g. fish omega-3
300 calories
17g. fat
7g. saturated fat

tuna & bacon hash browns

A real kick-start brunch. A food processor will make light work of grating the potato.

8oz. potatoes, grated
1 onion, finely chopped
8oz. tuna
4 smoked bacon rashers, chopped

2 eggs, beaten
2 tbsp. canola oil
salt
freshly ground black pepper

1 Put the potato in a pot of boiling water and cook 2 minutes. Drain, dry with paper towel and then tip it into a bowl and stir in the onion.
2 Heat the tuna 2 minutes in a nonstick pan over medium heat until opaque. Chop it coarsely and add it to the potato mix along with the bacon and egg. Season with salt and pepper, then use your hands to shape into 8 hash browns.
3 Heat the oil in a frying pan and fry the hash browns 5 minutes on each side, until lightly browned, then serve.

MAKES 4

PREPARATION + COOKING
15 + 15 minutes

STORAGE
This is not suitable for the refrigerator or freezer.

SERVE THIS WITH...
broiled tomatoes
freshly squeezed orange juice

OMEGA-3 SOURCES
Tuna, canola oil

NUTRITIONAL FACTS PER PORTION
0.6g. fish omega-3
0.8g. vegetarian omega-3
270 calories
16g. fat
3g. saturated fat

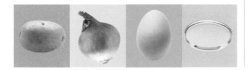

LUNCHES & LIGHT MEALS

Eat a lunch that keeps your mind and body productive all afternoon. Wholesome and stuffed with slow-release energy, omega-3 foods such as fish, beans, nuts, and seeds will power you through the day and fight mid-afternoon energy slumps. Pack a thermos of Three-Bean Tuscan Soup for a hearty lunch at your desk or enjoy a mouthwatering Seafood Phyllo Tart in your backyard. Many of these recipes, such as the deliciously light Watercress, Walnut, Pear & Roquefort Salad, can double as an accompaniment to a main meal, too, giving you even more opportunities to supercharge your body with omega-3.

three-bean tuscan soup

The trio of beans in this full-bodied Italian soup are packed with fiber and flavor.

SERVES 4

PREPARATION + COOKING
5 + 25 minutes

STORAGE
This will keep in the refrigerator for up to 3 days, or in the freezer for 3 months.

SERVE THIS WITH...
warm crusty bread
Tapenade Bruschetta
 (see page 58)

OMEGA-3 SOURCES
Canola oil, soybeans,
kidney beans, pinto beans

NUTRITION FACTS PER PORTION
1g. vegetarian omega-3
325 calories
10g. fat
1g. saturated fat

1 tbsp. canola oil
1 onion, chopped
3 garlic cloves, crushed
4½oz. pancetta, diced
4 tomatoes, roughly chopped
14oz. canned soybeans,
 drained
14oz. canned kidney beans,
 drained

7oz. canned pinto beans,
 drained
8oz. canned tomatoes, chopped
handful fresh basil, roughly
 chopped
2 vegetable stock cubes
1 tbsp. tomato paste
salt
freshly ground black pepper

1 Gently heat the oil in large heavy-based saucepan. Add the onion and cook 2 minutes until softened, then add the garlic, pancetta, and fresh tomatoes. Fry 2 to 3 minutes until softened.
2 Add the remaining ingredients, reserving a few sprigs of basil. Add 4⅓ cups water and simmer 20 minutes, stirring occasionally.
3 Season with salt and pepper and serve with the reserved basil.

hot & sour seafood soup

This soup is bursting with vibrant flavors—chili, garlic, tomato, and, of course, seafood.

1 tbsp. canola oil
1 small onion, chopped
1 garlic clove, crushed
1 red chili, chopped and deseeded
28oz. canned chopped tomatoes
¼ cup lemon juice

1 tbsp. sweet chill dipping sauce
7oz. cooked peeled jumbo shrimp
7oz. raw prepared squid, washed and chopped
3½oz. fresh egg noodles
2 tbsp. cilantro leaves, chopped

1 Heat the oil in a frying pan, add the onion, garlic, and chili and fry gently until soft. Add the tomatoes, lemon juice, and chili dipping sauce. Bring to the boil and cook 2 minutes until the liquid reduces by half.
2 Add the shrimp and squid. Bring back to a boil, add the noodles and cilantro, and cook 5 minutes, then serve.

SERVES 4

PREPARATION + COOKING
5 + 10 minutes

STORAGE
This can be kept in the refrigerator for 2 days.

SERVE THIS WITH...
low-fat shrimp crackers

OMEGA-3 SOURCES
Shrimp, squid, canola oil

NUTRITION FACTS PER PORTION
0.5g. fish omega-3
0.4g. vegetarian omega-3
225 calories
8g. fat
1.2g. saturated fat

salmon & broccoli chowder

A nutritious and delicious winter warmer, this chowder is super-charged with omega-3.

SERVES 4

PREPARATION + COOKING
10 + 30 minutes

STORAGE
This can be kept in the refrigerator for 3 days or frozen for up to 1 month.

SERVE THIS WITH...
Omega Bread (see page 72)

OMEGA-3 SOURCES
Salmon, canola oil

NUTRITION FACTS PER PORTION
2.5g. fish omega-3
0.4g. vegetarian omega-3
430 calories
22g. fat
5g. saturated fat

1 tbsp. canola oil
1 onion, chopped
1lb. 2oz. new potatoes, cut into 1in. chunks
2½ cups fish stock
5½oz. broccoli
1lb. 3oz. salmon fillets, skinned, boned, and cut into chunks
¼ cup canned corn
2 tbsp. chopped parsley
2 tbsp. chopped chives
2 tbsp. chopped mint
2 tbsp. reduced fat sour cream
salt
freshly ground black pepper

1 Heat the oil in a saucepan over medium heat. Add the onion and potatoes and cook 3 to 4 minutes until softened.

2 Add the stock and simmer 10 minutes. Add the broccoli, cover, and cook a further 10 minutes.

3 Add the salmon and corn and simmer 5 to 6 minutes, until the fish is cooked.

4 Remove from the heat, let cool 5 minutes, then stir in the herbs and sour cream. Season with salt and pepper and serve hot with some fresh bread.

fish soup

A low-fat, protein-rich, spicy winter soup.

1 tbsp. canola oil	1¼ cups tomato puree
2 garlic cloves, chopped	2½ cups fish stock
1 large onion, diced	5½oz. smoked haddock fillet
1 bay leaf	6oz. salmon fillet
⅓ cup white wine	1 tbsp. chopped parsley
½ tsp. chili flakes	4 tsp. crème fraîche
1½ tsp. oregano	freshly ground black pepper

1 Gently heat the oil in a deep saucepan. Add the garlic, onion, bay leaf, and wine and cook 5 minutes until the onion is translucent.

2 Add the chili flakes, oregano, and tomato puree and simmer 3 minutes. Add the fish stock and simmer a further 5 minutes.

3 Chop the fish fillets into ¾in. chunks and add to the pan. Cook over low heat 5 minutes.

4 Pour half the soup into a blender and let cool slightly before blending until smooth. Return to the pan and simmer 5 minutes until the fish is cooked.

5 Just before serving, stir in the parsley. Serve with a swirl of the crème fraîche and seasoned with pepper.

SERVES 4

PREPARATION + COOKING
10 + 25 minutes

STORAGE
Refrigerate for up to 3 days or freeze for up to 1 month.

SERVE THIS WITH...
crusty French bread or Omega Bread (see page 72)

OMEGA-3 SOURCES
Haddock, salmon, canola oil

NUTRITION FACTS PER PORTION
0.8g. fish omega-3
0.4g. vegetarian omega-3
210 calories
10g. fat
2g. saturated fat

V

watercress, walnut, pear & roquefort salad

SERVES 4

PREPARATION + COOKING
10 + 2 minutes

STORAGE
Store in an airtight jar for up to
1 week.

SERVE THIS WITH...
Honey Roast Salmon
 (see page 123)
Pissaladière (see page 115)

OMEGA-3 SOURCES
Walnuts, canola oil

NUTRITION FACTS PER PORTION
3.2g. vegetarian omega-3
450 calories
44g. fat
9.5g. saturated fat

Impressively rich in vegetarian omega-3, this
light and crunchy salad can be eaten either as
a main course or as an accompaniment.

scant ½ cup walnuts
5½oz. watercress
1 pear, peeled, cored, and
   thinly sliced
3oz. Roquefort cheese

Dressing:
¼ cup crème fraîche
⅓ cup canola oil
1oz. Roquefort cheese, grated
salt
freshly ground black pepper

1 Toast the walnuts 2 to 3 minutes under a hot broiler.
2 Meanwhile, whisk all the dressing ingredients together
in a bowl.
3 Mix the walnuts, watercress, and pear together in a
large bowl. Toss in the dressing, crumble the Roquefort
over the top, and serve.

Ⓥ ⓐ ⓑ ⓒ ⓓ

dressed green salad

A simple nutritious salad with a great mix of flavors. For an extra omega-3 hit, sprinkle it with a tablespoon of flax seeds.

1 tbsp. canola oil
1 slice of bread, crust removed and diced
3 cups spinach
3 cups arugula
3oz. cherry tomatoes, halved
1 avocado, peeled, pitted, and diced

Dressing:
2 tbsp. walnut oil
1 tbsp. lemon juice
1 tsp. clear honey
½ tsp. Dijon mustard
salt
freshly ground black pepper

1 Heat the oil in a frying pan, add the diced bread, and fry gently 1 to 2 minutes until golden. Drain the croutons on paper towel and set aside.

2 Whisk all the dressing ingredients together in a bowl and season with salt and pepper to taste.

3 Mix the salad ingredients together in a large bowl. Toss in the dressing and croutons and serve immediately.

SERVES 4

PREPARATION + COOKING
15 + 2 minutes

STORAGE
The dressing can be stored in the refrigerator for 1 week.

SERVE THIS WITH...
Tofu Mushrooms with Gruyère Crust (see page 52)

OMEGA-3 SOURCES
Spinach, arugula, canola oil, walnut oil

NUTRITION FACTS PER PORTION
1.3g. vegetarian omega-3
240 calories
21g. fat
3g. saturated fat

*five-spice tofu salad

OMEGA-3 SOURCES
Tofu, flax seed, canola oil, flax seed oil

NUTRITION FACTS PER PORTION
6g. vegetarian omega-3
335 calories
28g. fat
6g. saturated fat

Soy-rich foods such as tofu have been proven to help lower bad cholesterol levels. The extraordinary qualities of tofu include not only omega-3 protection for your heart, but also an ability to swiftly absorb other flavors—in this case, garlic, ginger, soy sauce, and Chinese five spice. Serve it on its own or as a virtuous accompaniment to a meal.

14oz. firm tofu, cut into ¾in. cubes
5½oz. mixed enoki, oyster, and button mushrooms, roughly chopped
3 handfuls mixed bok choy, bean sprouts, and shredded white cabbage
2 tbsp. canola oil
1 tsp. ground Chinese five spice

1 tbsp. whole flax seeds
handful cilantro leaves

Dressing:
½ cup crème fraîche
2 garlic cloves, crushed
¾in. gingerroot, grated
4 tbsp. mirin or sweet cider
1 tbsp. dark soy sauce
2 tbsp. flax seed oil

SERVES 4

PREPARATION + COOKING
15 + 3 minutes

STORAGE
The tofu mixture and dressing can be stored in the refrigerator for up to 3 days.

SERVE THIS WITH...
green tea
pineapple and mango fruit salad

1 Whisk all the dressing ingredients together in a bowl. Put the tofu and mushrooms in a large bowl, then pour the dressing over them. Let marinate 10 to 15 minutes.
2 Arrange the bok choy, bean sprouts, and cabbage on serving plates. Drain the the tofu and mushrooms, reserving the dressing. Heat the canola oil in a frying pan and add the tofu, mushrooms, five spice, and flax seeds. Stir-fry 2 to 3 minutes until lightly browned.
3 Top the greens with the tofu mixture, pour the reserved dressing over, sprinkle with the cilantro, and serve.

Try using smoked tofu for a slightly different flavor.

mixed bean salad

This colorful salad will leave you not only full of beans but also valuable omega-3.

SERVES 4

PREPARATION
10 minutes

STORAGE
This will keep in the refrigerator for 1 week.

SERVE THIS WITH...
Dolcelatte Tart (see page 50) or Parmesan Peppers with Balsamic Tofu (see page 91)

OMEGA-3 SOURCES
soybeans, pinto beans, black beans, kidney beans, canola oil, flax seed oil

NUTRITION FACTS PER PORTION
4g. vegetarian omega-3
340 calories
16g. fat
1.4g. saturated fat

½ cup canned soybeans, drained
½ cup canned pinto beans, drained
½ cup canned black beans, drained
¾ cup canned kidney beans, drained

Dressing:
2 tbsp. balsamic vinegar
2 tbsp. canola oil
2 tbsp. flax seed oil
handful chopped parsley
½ tsp. coarse ground mustard
salt
freshly ground black pepper

1 Whisk all the dressing ingredients together in a bowl and season with salt and pepper.
2 Mix the beans together in a large bowl.
3 Add the dressing to the beans, mix well, and serve.

crab, avocado & jumbo shrimp salad

The light citrus dressing offsets the richness of the crab in this luxurious seafood salad.

9oz. whole crab meat
16 cooked, peeled jumbo shrimp
2 avocados, peeled, pitted, and diced
4 large handfuls mixed salad greens
freshly ground black pepper

Dressing:
4 tbsp. olive oil
4 tbsp. lemon juice
2 garlic cloves, crushed
½ tsp. paprika
salt
freshly ground black pepper

1 To make the dressing, whisk the ingredients together in a bowl and season with salt and pepper to taste.
2 Put the crab meat in a bowl and add the shrimp. Pour in the dressing and stir well.
3 Gently stir the avocado into the crab mixture.
4 Arrange the salad greens with the crab mixture, season with pepper, and serve immediately.

SERVES 4

PREPARATION
10 minutes

STORAGE
This dish is not suitable for the refrigerator or freezer.

SERVE THIS WITH...
Seeded Flatbread (see page 70)

OMEGA-3 SOURCES
Crab, shrimp

NUTRITION FACTS PER PORTION
0.9g. fish omega-3
370 calories
29g. fat
5.5g. saturated fat

022

smoked trout & horseradish salad

SERVES 4

PREPARATION + COOKING
5 + 15 minutes

STORAGE
This will keep in the refrigerator for 2 days.

SERVE THIS WITH...
watercress
sliced tomatoes

OMEGA-3 SOURCES
Trout

NUTRITION FACTS PER PORTION
0.7g. fish omega-3
323 calories
17g. fat
4g. saturated fat

Horseradish and smoked trout are a great pairing. They combine with this creamy dressing, made lighter by using crème fraîche.

1lb. 5oz. new potatoes
2 heaped tsp. grated
  horseradish
¼ cup mayonnaise
¼ cup crème fraîche
1 small red onion, finely sliced
9oz. hot-smoked trout fillets
2 tsp. chopped parsley

1 Boil the potatoes 15 minutes until just soft, then drain and cut them in half. Set aside to cool.
2 In a bowl, mix together the horseradish, mayonnaise, and crème fraîche.
3 Add the potatoes and onion to the bowl and mix so that they are coated with the creamy dressing.
4 Flake the trout into the bowl and carefully mix well. Sprinkle with the chopped parsley and serve.

salmon & potato salad

This summer dish has a chic retro vibe.

14oz. fresh salmon
1 cup fish stock
scant ½ cup horseradish sauce
1 x ¼oz. envelope gelatin
3 tbsp. chopped dill
1 garlic clove
1 tbsp. lemon juice
1 tsp. olive oil
8oz. smoked salmon slices

freshly ground black pepper
handful watercress sprigs

New Potato Salad:
1lb. new potatoes, scrubbed
    and halved
2 tbsp. chives
2 tbsp. olive oil
4 tbsp. sour cream

1 Put the salmon in a saucepan with enough stock to cover the fish and poach 10 minutes. Then remove the salmon from the stock and set aside. Meanwhile, boil the new potatoes 15 minutes until tender.
2 Add the horseradish sauce to the pan of stock. Add the gelatin and dissolve over low heat. Add the dill, garlic, lemon juice, black pepper, and the poached, flaked salmon.
3 Mix the boiled potatoes with the chives, oil, and cream.
4 Grease an 8in. ring mold with the olive oil and line it with the smoked salmon slices. Fill the mold with the cooled salmon and horseradish filling, then transfer it to the refrigerator to set. This will take about 3 hours.
5 Turn out onto a serving plate. Fill the center with the potato salad and garnish with the sprigs of watercress.

SERVES 4

PREPARATION + COOKING
30 + 20 minutes
+ setting

STORAGE
This will keep in the refrigerator for up to 3 days.

SERVE THIS WITH...
Dressed Green Salad
  (see page 43)

OMEGA-3 SOURCES
Salmon

NUTRITION FACTS PER PORTION
3g. fish omega-3
490 calories
28g. fat
6g. saturated fat

dolcelatte tart

Dolcelatte cheese is fabulous melted. Its slight saltiness works perfectly with walnuts.

SERVES 6

PREPARATION + COOKING
20 + 15 minutes

STORAGE
Keep in the refrigerator for 3 days. Not suitable for freezing.

OMEGA-3 SOURCES
Canola oil, walnuts, ground flax seed

SERVE THIS WITH...
tomato salad

NUTRITION FACTS PER PORTION
3.3g. vegetarian omega-3
410 calories
31g. fat
9.5g. saturated fat

2 tbsp. canola oil
2 red bell peppers, deseeded
    and sliced into strips
1 egg white
½ cup crème fraîche
6oz. Dolcelatte, crumbled
scant ½ cup walnuts, chopped
1 tsp. chopped thyme
salt
freshly ground black pepper

Pastry:
1 cup all-purpose flour
½ cup ground flax seed
pinch of salt
¼ cup olive oil spread
1 egg yolk
3 to 4 tbsp. water

1 Preheat the oven to 425°F. Put the flour, flax seed, and salt in a bowl. Rub in the olive oil spread. Add the egg yolk and 3 or 4 tablespoons water to bind the pastry. Knead briefly, wrap in plastic wrap, and chill 30 minutes.
2 Pour the oil over the peppers and roast 15 minutes.
3 Whisk the egg white until it is frothy but not stiff. Fold in the crème fraîche and Dolcelatte. Season with salt and pepper and put in the refrigerator.
4 Roll out the pastry. Cut out a 9in. circle, place on a nonstick baking sheet, and prick with a fork. Cover with the Dolcelatte mixture, peppers, and walnuts. Sprinkle with thyme and bake 15 minutes until golden.

walnut & arugula pesto pasta

A novel twist on a classic pesto sauce to enhance its omega-3 levels.

2 cups dried penne pasta
scant ½ cup walnuts, chopped
2 tbsp. Parmesan, to serve

Walnut Pesto:
2 large handfuls arugula
handful basil
1 tbsp. walnut oil
2 garlic cloves
1 tsp. salt
²/₃ cup grated Parmesan

1 Boil a pot of water, add the pasta, and cook 10 minutes or according to the packet instructions.
2 Meanwhile, toast the walnuts under a hot broiler.
3 Briefly whizz the arugula and basil in a blender. Add the oil, garlic, salt, and Parmesan and blend well.
4 Drain the pasta and return it to the pot. Stir in the pesto and serve sprinkled with a little Parmesan cheese.

SERVES 4

COOKING + PREPARATION
5 + 15 minutes

STORAGE
The walnut pesto will keep for up to 1 week in the refrigerator.

SERVE THIS WITH...
Easy Salmon & Pesto Quiche
(see page 109)

OMEGA-3 SOURCES
Walnuts, arugula, walnut oil

NUTRITION FACTS PER PORTION
1.5g. vegetarian omega-3
450 calories
19g. fat
4g. saturated fat

026

V 🐟 🐸 🍽

tofu mushrooms with gruyère crust

Omega-3 comes in a variety of guises in this filling dish—tofu, hemp, and canola oil.

SERVES 4

PREPARATION + COOKING
15 + 20 minutes

STORAGE
Store, covered, in the refrigerator for up to 3 days.

SERVE THIS WITH...
Dressed Green Salad
(see page 43)

OMEGA-3 SOURCES
Tofu, hemp seeds, and oil, canola oil

NUTRITION FACTS PER PORTION
3.1g. vegetarian omega-3
530 calories
40g. fat
13g. saturated fat

½ cup hemp seeds
1 cup Gruyère cheese, grated
8 portobello mushrooms, wiped
    and stalks removed
2 tbsp. canola oil
1lb. firm tofu
¼ cup tomato puree

2 tbsp. tomato paste
2 tbsp. hemp oil
1 cup finely chopped Gruyère
    cheese
2 handfuls basil, chopped
salt
freshly ground black pepper

1 Preheat the oven to 375°F. Toast the hemp seeds in a hot dry pan over medium heat 2 minutes, then grind them using a mortar and pestle or a blender. Add the grated cheese, season, and set aside.

2 Brush the mushrooms with the canola oil and place them on a baking sheet.

3 Mix together the remaining ingredients using a fork.

4 Stuff the mushrooms, dividing the tofu mixture equally. Top each mushroom with a quarter of the hemp seed topping. Bake 15 to 20 minutes until browned, then serve.

Ⓥ ⓐ Ⓞ Ⓞ ⓐ ⓑ

soy & hemp falafels

Traditionally made with chickpeas, this version uses soy protein and hemp for a nuttier taste.

scant 1 cup textured soy protein	½ cup hemp seeds
2 tbsp. canola oil	¼ cup ground flax seed
1 small red onion, finely diced	¼ cup all-purpose flour
1 tsp. chili powder	2 eggs, beaten
½ tsp. paprika	salt
1 red bell pepper, finely diced	freshly ground black pepper

1 Soak the soy protein in 1¼ cups warm water 5 to 10 minutes or according to the packet instructions.
2 Heat half the oil in a pan, add the onion, chili powder, and paprika, and fry a few minutes. Add the pepper and fry 5 minutes until softened.
3 Meanwhile, toast the hemp seeds under a hot broiler 2 minutes, then grind them as finely possible using a mortar and pestle or a blender.
4 Add the soy and hemp to the onion mixture, stir well, and season with salt and pepper. Add the ground flax seed, flour, and eggs. Using your hands, shape the mixture into 12 balls.
5 Heat the remaining oil in a pan and lightly fry the falafels for 10 minutes until browned all over, then serve.

SERVES 4

PREPARATION + COOKING
15 + 15 minutes

STORAGE
The cooked falafels will keep for 3 to 4 days in the refrigerator.

SERVE THIS WITH...
Seeded Flatbread (see page 70)
shredded lettuce
plain yogurt

OMEGA-3 SOURCES
Canola oil, hemp seeds, ground flax seed

NUTRITION FACTS PER PORTION
4.1g. vegetarian omega-3
290 calories
18g. fat
2g. saturated fat

hummus

This recipe makes a hummus that is much higher in vegetarian omega-3 than the conventional type. It makes a great dip or sandwich filler.

SERVES 4

PREPARATION
5 minutes

STORAGE
This will keep in the refrigerator for up to 3 days, or it can be frozen for up to 1 month.

SERVE THIS WITH...
pita bread
celery sticks
carrot batons

OMEGA-3 SOURCES
Soybeans, flax seed oil

NUTRITION FACTS PER PORTION
3.2g. vegetarian omega-3
180 calories
16g. fat
2.3g. saturated fat

¹⁄₃ cup canned soybeans
¼ cup canned chickpeas
1½ tsp. tahini paste
1½ tsp. flax seed oil
1½ tsp. olive oil

1 tbsp. crème fraîche
1 garlic clove, crushed
juice and zest of ½ lemon
salt
freshly ground black pepper

1 Blend all the ingredients in a food processor or with a hand blender. Stop when they reach the consistency you prefer—smooth or coarse.
2 Serve chilled or at room temperature.

sardine polenta patties

Sardines are highly nutritious and full of flavor. The flavors of cilantro and lemon give them a really fresh twist.

3 large handfuls spinach
4½oz. canned sardines in
   tomato sauce
14oz. ready-made polenta
1 egg
large handful cilantro
juice and zest of 1 lemon
¼ cup all-purpose flour

2 tbsp. canola oil
salt
freshly ground black pepper

Lemon Dressing:
scant ½ cup crème fraîche
1 tbsp. lemon juice
freshly ground black pepper

1 Steam the spinach in a double boiler 2 minutes, then blend it with all the patty ingredients, except the flour and oil, in a food processor. Season with salt and pepper.
2 Whisk the dressing ingredients together in a bowl, season with pepper, then set aside in the refrigerator.
3 Shape the polenta mixture into four patties. Put the flour in a shallow bowl, then carefully coat each patty generously with flour. The mixture will be soft and pliable, so be careful not to over-handle it. The patties can be set aside at this stage, if desired.
4 Heat the oil in a pan and fry each patty 5 to 7 minutes over medium heat until browned, turning only once during cooking. Serve hot with the lemon dressing.

SERVES 4

PREPARATION + COOKING
10 + 10 minutes

STORAGE
This will keep in the refrigerator for 2 days.

SERVE THIS WITH...
a crisp salad
coleslaw

OMEGA-3 SOURCES
Sardines, spinach, canola oil

NUTRITION FACTS PER PORTION
0.5g. fish omega-3
0.8g. vegetarian omega-3
310 calories
21g. fat
8g. saturated fat

anchovy tapas rolls

PREPARATION
5 minutes

STORAGE
These will keep in the refrigerator for 2 days.

SERVE THIS WITH...
Shrimp and Chorizo Tapas
(see page 57)

OMEGA-3 SOURCES
Anchovies

NUTRITION FACTS PER PORTION
1g. fish omega-3
140 calories
10g. fat
0.2g. saturated fat

These quick bites are ideal as part of a tapas selection. Fresh anchovies are quite different from their saltier canned counterparts. Together with the olives, tomatoes, and gherkins, they make a delicious Mediterranean medley.

24 fresh anchovy fillets
8 whole black or green olives
8 cherry tomatoes
8 gherkins

1 Roll the fresh anchovy fillets around each of the different fillings, securing each with a toothpick.
2 Chill or serve immediately.

shrimp & chorizo tapas

This is a quick and easy snack or appetizer. It looks great served in a traditional earthenware tapas bowl.

¼ cup canola oil
7oz. cooked, peeled shrimp
4oz. chorizo sausage, sliced

4 garlic cloves, crushed
4 large slices fresh crusty bread

1 Preheat the oven to 425°F. Measure the oil into an ovenproof dish and warm in the oven 5 minutes.
2 Add the shrimp, sausage, and garlic to the oil and return the dish to the oven. Bake 10 minutes. Serve immediately with fresh crusty bread—great for dipping.

SERVES 4

PREPARATION + COOKING
5 + 10 minutes

STORAGE
This dish is not suitable for the refrigerator or freezer.

SERVE THIS WITH…
Anchovy Tapas Rolls
  (see page 56)
Crab Cakes (see page 100)

OMEGA-3 SOURCES
Shrimp, canola oil

NUTRITION FACTS PER PORTION
1.5g. fish omega-3
 0.3g. vegetarian omega-3
350 calories
23g. fat
4g. saturated fat

032

tapenade bruschetta

Tapenade is a classic Provençal spread traditionally served on rustic breads or used as a stuffing. Here it is combined with French bread for a tasty snack or appetizer.

SERVES 4

PREPARATION
15 minutes

STORAGE
The tapenade will keep in a jar in the refrigerator for up to a week.

SERVE THIS WITH...
Three-Bean Tuscan Soup
 (see page 38)

OMEGA-3 SOURCES
Anchovies, hemp oil

NUTRITION FACTS PER PORTION
0.3g. fish omega-3
1.5g. vegetarian omega-3
540 calories
22g. fat
4.6g. saturated fat

1½ cups pitted black olives
¾ cup capers
2¼oz. canned anchovy fillets,
 drained
2 tbsp. lemon juice
1 tsp. wholegrain mustard

2 tbsp. hemp oil
12 large slices of French bread
2 garlic cloves
4 tomatoes, chopped
freshly ground black pepper

1 To make the tapenade, put the olives, capers, anchovies, lemon juice, mustard, and oil in a blender and mix until quite smooth.

2 Lightly toast the French bread. Halve the garlic cloves and rub them over the slices of toast.

3 Spread the tapenade over the bread, top with the chopped tomato, and season liberally with pepper, then serve.

hot-smoked trout pâté

This pâté is an excellent starter and, being perfectly portable, is ideal for a summer picnic.

4½oz. hot-smoked trout fillets
3 tsp. horseradish sauce
2 tbsp. crème fraîche

zest of ½ lemon
dill sprigs, to serve

1 In a bowl, mash the trout fillets with a fork.
2 Add the horseradish sauce and crème fraîche and mix well.
3 Stir in the lemon zest and mix well. Scatter a few sprigs of dill over the top and serve.

SERVES 4

PREPARATION
5 minutes

STORAGE
This will keep for 1 day in the refrigerator.

SERVE THIS WITH...
Oatcakes (see page 71)

OMEGA-3 SOURCES
Trout

NUTRITION FACTS PER PORTION
0.3g. fish omega-3
50 calories
3g. fat
1g. saturated fat

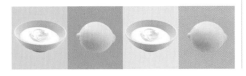

smoked mackerel dip

SERVES 4

PREPARATION
5 minutes

STORAGE
Cover, refrigerate, and eat within 3 days.

SERVE THIS WITH...
sesame seed breadsticks
sliced carrots
Oatcakes (see page 71)

OMEGA-3 SOURCES
Mackerel

NUTRITION FACTS PER PORTION
0.7g. fish omega-3
100 calories
8g. fat
3.4g. saturated fat

This classic dip is surprisingly popular with children—great news for parents, as it is bursting with fish omega-3. Serve it either with a selection of chopped vegetables and breadsticks or as a nutritious sandwich filling.

3½oz. smoked mackerel fillet
scant ½ cup crème fraîche
juice of 1 lime

salt
freshly ground black pepper

1 Peel the skin off the back of the mackerel fillet and break the flesh up into small pieces with a fork.
2 Add the crème fraîche and lime juice, season with salt and pepper, and mix together until it reaches the desired consistency.
3 Chill or serve immediately.

smoked mackerel & spinach tartlets

For quick, nutritious, and tasty canapés, these are perfect. Conveniently, they can be made in advance and chilled for up to 2 days, too.

5 tbsp. canola oil
10 slices of wholewheat bread
4 large handfuls spinach
7oz. cream cheese

4½oz. smoked mackerel fillets, flaked
⅓ cup grated Parmesan cheese
freshly ground black pepper

SERVES 10

PREPARATION + COOKING
5 + 20 minutes

STORAGE
These canapés can be kept in an airtight container in the refrigerator for up to 2 days.

SERVE THIS WITH...
cherry tomatoes
Tapenade Bruschetta
  (see page 58)

OMEGA-3 SOURCES
Canola oil, spinach, mackerel

NUTRITION FACTS PER PORTION
0.3g. fish omega-3
0.8g. vegetarian omega-3
260 calories
20g. fat
7.4g. saturated fat

1 Heat the oven to 400°F. Generously grease a muffin pan with the canola oil.

2 Using a small cookie cutter, cut 2 rounds of bread out of each slice and press the bread rounds into the pan to make the tartlet shells. Bake 8 minutes while preparing the filling.

3 To make the filling, steam the spinach in a double boiler, for 3–4 minutes then drain and mix together with the cream cheese and mackerel. Season with pepper.

4 When ready, remove the tartlet shells from the oven and divide the filling between them. Top with the Parmesan cheese and bake the tartlets a further 8 to 10 minutes, or until they are lightly browned all over.

OMEGA-3 SOURCES
Crab, shrimp, canola oil

NUTRITION FACTS PER PORTION
0.9g. fish omega-3
0.2g. vegetarian omega-3
220 calories
7g. fat
2.1g. saturated fat

seafood phyllo tarts

The crab and shrimp in these tarts are not only good sources of omega-3 but also full of flavor. The brown crab meat is found in the crab's main shell, while the white meat is from the claws. Fortunately, if time is short, ready-prepared shrimp and crab meat are widely available.

1½ tsp. canola oil
4½oz. fresh crab (including
  brown meat)
2 tbsp. crème fraîche
1 tbsp. lemon juice
4oz. cooked, peeled shrimp

4 sheets phyllo dough
¼ cup milk
4 lime wedges, to serve
salt
freshly ground black pepper

SERVES 4

PREPARATION + COOKING
10 + 15 minutes

STORAGE
Store in the refrigerator
overnight and eat the following
day. Not suitable for freezing.

1 Preheat the oven to 350°F. Using the oil, grease four
4½in. tart pans.

2 Spoon the crab, crème fraîche, lemon juice, and shrimp
into a food processor and process for a few seconds until
well mixed. Season with salt and pepper.

3 Remove the phyllo sheets from the roll and lay them out
on a clean surface. Cut the sheets into four squares. Place
each square on top of the tart pans and fan the layers out.
Brush with milk to soften the dough.

4 Divide the mixture between the tart pans and gently
push the dough down into the pans. Brush with milk and
bake 15 minutes until golden brown. Serve warm with
a green salad and the lime wedges.

SERVE THIS WITH...
Dressed Green Salad
  (see page 43)
melon wedges

Unwrap the phyllo
dough at the last
minute to prevent
it from drying out.

● ● ○ ○

smoked salmon tarts

An innovative recipe, the twist to these tarts is that they need no dough!

SERVES 4

PREPARATION + COOKING
10 + 15 minutes

STORAGE
Keep refrigerated and eat within
2 days.

SERVE THIS WITH...
Mixed Bean Salad (see page 46)

OMEGA-3 SOURCES
Salmon, canola oil, spinach,
arugula

NUTRITION FACTS PER PORTION
1.2g. fish omega-3
0.8g. vegetarian omega-3
210 calories
14g fat
4g. saturated fat

7oz. smoked salmon
2 tbsp. canola oil
4 eggs
½ cup crème fraîche
2 tsp. lemon juice

large handful watercress,
spinach, or arugula,
chopped
freshly ground black pepper

1 Preheat the oven to 400°C. Cut the salmon into 1¼in.-wide strips. Put eight lightly greased paper baking cups in a muffin pan.
2 Line each one with a single layer of salmon strips so that there are no gaps.
3 In a bowl, whisk the eggs. Add the crème fraîche and lemon juice, mix in the greens, and season with pepper.
4 Spoon the mixture into the muffin pan and bake 15 minutes, or until the filling is firm to the touch.
5 Let the tarts cool slightly, then remove them from the pan and serve.

smoked salmon & goat cheese bagels

A delicious way to serve smoked salmon, the honey and mustard dressing perfectly complements the rich goat cheese.

2 bagels, halved
4 slices of smoked salmon
7oz. goat cheese, sliced into
   8 rounds

4 tsp. clear honey
1 tsp. Dijon mustard

1 Lightly toast the bagels under a hot broiler. Place a slice of salmon on each bagel half and top with two slices of goat cheese.

2 Return the bagel halves to the broiler 3 to 4 minutes until the cheese starts to bubble and brown.

3 Meanwhile, mix the honey and mustard together.

4 Drizzle the dressing over the bagels and serve warm.

SERVES 4

PREPARATION + COOKING
5 + 10 minutes

STORAGE
This is not suitable for the refrigerator or freezer.

SERVE THIS WITH...
lemon wedges

OMEGA-3 SOURCES
Salmon

NUTRITION FACTS PER PORTION
0.6g. fish omega-3
280 calories
15g. fat
9g. saturated fat

SERVES 4

PREPARATION + COOKING
65 + 15 minutes

STORAGE
This dish is unsuitable for the refrigerator or freezer.

SERVE THIS WITH...
Spicy Tuna Burgers
(see page 116)

OMEGA-3 SOURCES
Sardines

NUTRITION FACTS PER PORTION
1.7g. fish omega-3
300 calories
32g. fat
4g. saturated fat

marinated sardine & tomato skewers

The aroma of these barbecued sardines is guaranteed to evoke the Mediterranean.

16 fresh sardine fillets
16 cherry tomatoes

Marinade:
2 tbsp. olive oil

2 tbsp. white wine vinegar
1 tbsp. lemon juice
1 garlic clove, crushed
freshly ground black pepper

1 To make the marinade, whisk the oil, vinegar, lemon juice, and garlic together in a bowl. Season with pepper.

2 Lay the sardines in a dish, pour the marinade over them, cover, and chill in the refrigerator 1 hour.

3 Remove the sardines from the marinade and pat dry on paper towel. Wrap each fillet around a tomato and thread onto a skewer. Use 4 fillets per skewer.

4 Cook under a hot broiler or on a hot barbecue 3 to 4 minutes, turning halfway through. Serve immediately.

tandoori trout wraps

The tandoori paste really lifts the flavor of the trout without being too strong.

14oz. trout fillets
3 tbsp. tandoori paste
¼ cup crème fraîche
4 flour tortillas

2 tbsp. mayonnaise
2 handfuls salad greens
½ cucumber, sliced

1 Lay the trout fillets in a baking dish.

2 In a small bowl, stir together 2 tablespoons of the tandoori paste and all the crème fraîche. Spread this over the trout, cover with plastic wrap, and chill in the refrigerator to marinate at least 30 minutes.

3 Preheat the oven to 400°F. Remove the plastic wrap and cook the marinated trout fillets in the top of the oven 20 minutes.

4 Remove the fillets from the oven and place them on a chopping board. While cooling, mix together the remaining tandoori paste and the mayonnaise and spread this over the tortilla wraps.

5 Remove the trout skins, flake the flesh into large chunks, and lay them on top of the tortilla wraps. Top with the salad and cucumber and roll up. Cut on the diagonal and serve.

SERVES 4

PREPARATION + COOKING
30 + 25 minutes

STORAGE
This will keep in the refrigerator for 2 days.

SERVE THIS WITH...
plain naan bread instead
  of tortillas

OMEGA-3 SOURCES
Trout

NUTRITION FACTS PER PORTION
1.1g. fish omega-3
0.2g. vegetarian omega-3
285 calories
15g. fat
3.5g. saturated fat

SNACKS

The trick to healthy snacking is to plan ahead. Deliciously decadent, but with a healthy omega-3 twist, Chocolate & Walnut Muffins are pretty much irresistible and easily fill a rumbling tummy. Slip an Oat Bar or some Hemp & Honey Cookies into your children's lunchboxes knowing that the hidden omega-3 may aid their concentration and even good behavior. Afternoon treats such as lighter-than-air Frosted Cupcakes or moist Date & Walnut Loaf are so easy to make you'll wonder why you don't bake more regularly. And for bread-lovers, try the incredible Omega Bread—it not only tastes amazing, but also fills your kitchen with the most delicious freshly baked aroma.

Ⓥ ⓐ ⓓ ⓖ ⓢ

seeded flatbread

This easy flatbread is great served warm from the pan. So long as you use a good proportion of omega-3-rich hemp seeds, you can use any seeds that you have available.

SERVES 6

PREPARATION + COOKING
10 + 8 minutes + resting

STORAGE
Best served immediately, but will keep in an airtight container for 2–3 days.

SERVE THIS WITH...
Three-Bean Tuscan Soup
(see page 38)

OMEGA-3 SOURCES
Hemp seeds, flax seed oil, hemp oil

NUTRITION FACTS PER PORTION
2.1g. vegetarian omega-3
155 calories
7g. fat
0.9g. saturated fat

2 tbsp. hemp seeds
2 tbsp. poppy seeds
1¼ cups all-purpose flour
1 tsp. baking powder

½ tsp. salt
1 tbsp. flax seed oil
1 tbsp. hemp oil

1 Set a frying pan over medium heat and toast the seeds 2 to 3 minutes until they start to brown. Then grind them in a mortar and pestle.
2 Sift the flour, baking powder, and sea salt into a bowl. Add the ground seeds and flax seed oil. Stirring with a wooden spoon, drizzle in ½ cup boiling water, or just enough to form a dough.
3 Knead on a floured surface 2 minutes, then wrap the dough in plastic wrap and set aside to rest 20 minutes.
4 Roll out the dough until it is ½in. thick. Heat the hemp oil in a frying pan and gently fry the dough 3 to 4 minutes on each side until golden. Place a lid on the pan to help cook the bread thoroughly. Cut the bread into 6 pieces and serve immediately.

Ⓥ ⓐ ⓑ ⓒ

oatcakes

Oatcakes, a traditional Scottish staple, are an excellent snack to keep you going on busy days. They are really simple and quick to make, plus they fill your kitchen with a delicious oaty smell as they bake.

1 heaping cup rolled oats
¼ cup ground flax seed
½ tsp. salt

pinch of baking soda
1 tbsp. canola oil

1 Preheat the oven to 350°F. Put the oats in a food processor and pulse until coarsely ground.
2 Put the oats, flax seed, salt, and baking soda in a large bowl. Stir in the oil and 2 tbsp. hot water and press together to make a firm dough.
3 Roll out on a lightly floured surface and use a 3in. round cookie cutter to cut out 8 oatcakes, rerolling as necessary.
4 Bake 8 to 10 minutes, or until golden and crisp.

MAKES 8

PREPARATION + COOKING
10 + 10 minutes

STORAGE
Store in an airtight container for up to 2 weeks.

SERVE THIS WITH...
Smoked Mackerel Dip
(see page 60)
Hot Smoked Trout Pâté
(see page 59)

OMEGA-3 SOURCES
Ground flax seed, canola oil

NUTRITION FACTS PER PORTION
1.1g. vegetarian omega-3
100 calories
6g. fat
0.3g. saturated fat

043

OMEGA 3 SOURCES
Flax seed, hemp oil, walnuts

NUTRITION FACTS PER SLICE
3.0g. vegetarian omega-3
280 calories
12g. fat
1.3g. saturated fat

omega bread

Made with flax seeds, hemp oil, and walnuts, this nutritious bread is packed with omega-3 and releases energy slowly, so you won't need to snack between meals. Vegetarian omega-3 fats are essential for promoting heart health, particularly for those who don't eat fish.

1½ tsp. canola oil
3 cups white bread flour, plus
extra for kneading
¾ cup wholewheat bread flour
½ cup ground flax seed
2 tbsp. hemp oil
1½ tsp. salt
1½ tsp. sugar

1 heaped tsp. active dried
yeast
⅔ cup walnuts, toasted and
crushed
½ cup flax seed, plus extra to
decorate
¼ cup pumpkin seeds, plus
extra to decorate

SERVES 12

PREPARATION + COOKING
20 + 45 minutes + rising

STORAGE
This bread can be frozen for up
to 1 month.

SERVE THIS WITH...
sharp cheddar cheese
walnuts
chutney

1 Preheat the oven to 350°F. Grease a 2lb. loaf pan with the canola oil.

2 Mix together the flours and ground flax seed. Add the oil, salt, sugar, yeast, nuts, and seeds. Gradually add 1½ cups warm water to make a pliable dough (you may not need it all). Knead on a floured surface 10 minutes.

3 Let the dough rise under a clean damp cloth 30 minutes, then knead 5 minutes and shape to fit the loaf pan. Leave in a warm place under a clean damp cloth 45 minutes, or until doubled in size.

4 Decorate with seeds and bake 45 minutes, or until the loaf sounds hollow when tapped. Serve warm or cold.

You can also
use this dough
to make rolls,
which take just
40 minutes
to bake.

walnut & banana bread

This popular afternoon treat can also double as a healthy addition to a lunch box.

SERVES 12

PREPARATION + COOKING
15 + 30 minutes

STORAGE
Store in an airtight container for up to 2 weeks or freeze for up to 1 month.

SERVE THIS WITH...
cream cheese

OMEGA-3 SOURCES
Canola oil, walnut oil, walnuts

NUTRITION FACTS PER PORTION
1.8g. vegetarian omega-3
275 calories
18g. fat
2g. saturated fat

1½ tsp. canola oil
3 soft ripe bananas, peeled
6 tbsp. olive oil spread
6 tbsp. walnut oil
juice and grated zest of
    1 orange
¾ cup all-purpose flour
¾ cup wholemeal pastry flour
¼ cup brown sugar
1 tsp. baking soda
1 tsp. pumpkin pie spice
3 eggs
1 cup walnuts, chopped

1 Preheat the oven to 375°F. Using the canola oil, grease and line a 2lb. loaf pan.
2 Mash the bananas in a large mixing bowl. Mix in the olive oil spread, walnut oil, and orange juice and zest.
3 Gradually add all the remaining ingredients, except the walnuts. Do this slowly to prevent the eggs from curdling. Fold in the walnuts.
4 Pour the mixture into the loaf pan and bake 30 minutes, or until a skewer comes out clean.

(V) (◉) (O) (◉) (◉) (◉) (◉) (◉)

chocolate & walnut muffins

What use is virtue without a little vice? The addition of a few chocolate chunks make these delicious muffins sinfully good.

2 eggs
²/₃ cup milk
6 tbsp. hemp oil
1 tsp. vanilla extract
1¹/₃ heaping cups self-rising
    flour
heaping ²/₃ cup wholewheat
    pastry flour

¼ cup ground flax seed
1 tbsp. baking powder
heaping ¼ cup unrefined sugar
3oz. dark chocolate, broken
    into chunks
scant ½ cup walnuts, chopped
½ cup raisins

1 Preheat the oven to 400°F. Place 12 paper baking cups in a muffin pan.
2 Whisk together the eggs, milk, oil, and vanilla extract.
3 In a bowl, sift together the flours, ground flax seed, and baking powder, adding back the bran from the flour. Stir in the sugar and make a well in the middle.
4 Slowly pour in the liquid mixture, stirring all the time to make a thick batter. Do not beat. Fold in the chocolate chunks, walnuts, and raisins until well mixed.
5 Divide the mixture into the muffin pan and bake 20 minutes, or until golden brown.

MAKES 12

PREPARATION + COOKING
10 + 20 minutes

STORAGE
Store in an airtight container for up to a week.

SERVE THIS WITH...
ice cream

OMEGA-3 SOURCES
Hemp oil, ground flax seed, walnuts

NUTRITION FACTS PER PORTION
2.2g. vegetarian omega-3
264 calories
15g. fat
2.9g. saturated fat

oatbars

These bars are great as a snack and perfect to add to the lunchbox or picnic basket.

MAKES 12

PREPARATION + COOKING
5 + 25 minutes

STORAGE
Store in an airtight container for up to a week.

SERVE THIS WITH...
fruit salad

OMEGA-3 SOURCES
Canola oil, ground flax seed, walnuts

NUTRITION FACTS PER PORTION
0.8g. vegetarian omega-3
200 calories
12g. fat
5g. saturated fat

½ tsp. canola oil
scant ½ cup olive oil spread
heaping ¼ cup unrefined sugar
2 tbsp. runny honey
2 tbsp. light corn syrup

1½ cups oats
¼ cup ground flax seed
scant ½ cup walnuts, chopped
½ cup raisins

1 Preheat the oven to 350°F. Grease a shallow baking pan with the oil.

2 Melt the olive oil spread in a pan. Add the sugar, honey, and light corn syrup.

3 Mix the oats, flax seed, and walnuts together and add them to the butter mixture. Add the raisins and stir well.

4 Pour into the baking pan and spread out to about 1in. deep. Bake 20 to 25 minutes.

5 Remove from the oven and let cool 10 minutes. Cut into bar shapes in the pan. Let cool before removing them from the pan and serving.

Ⓥ ⊚ ⓞ ⊘ ⊘ ⊛ ⊛

coconut & cherry squares

Sweet, sticky, and slightly chewy, these squares are predictably popular.

scant 1 cup canola oil
¾ cup sugar
1¹/₃ cups all-purpose flour
2 eggs
½ cup ground flax seed
2 tsp. baking powder
¹/₃ cup shredded coconut

¼ cup candied cherries, chopped

Topping:
scant 1½ cups powdered sugar
¹/₃ cup shredded coconut
8 candied cherries, halved, to decorate

MAKES 16

PREPARATION + COOKING
10 + 35 minutes

STORAGE
This will keep in an airtight container for 5 days or un-iced in the freezer for up to 3 months.

SERVE THIS WITH...
cherries

OMEGA-3 SOURCES
Canola oil, ground flax seed

NUTRITION FACTS PER PORTION
1.8g. vegetarian omega-3
274 calories
15g. fat
2.8g. saturated fat

1 Preheat the oven to 325°F. Using 1½ teaspoons of the canola oil, grease and line a 9in. square cake pan.
2 In a mixing bowl, mix together the oil, sugar, flour, eggs, flax seed, and baking powder until smooth. Stir in the coconut and cherries, and pour into the cake pan. Bake 30 to 35 minutes.
3 Remove the cake from the pan and let cool before icing. Mix the powdered sugar with 3 tablespoons water, adding a little at a time until it's runny enough to drip off a spoon. Spread over the cake, sprinkle with coconut, and slice into 16 squares. Top each square with a cherry half and serve.

hemp & honey cookies

The nutty flavor of the hemp seeds belies the fact that these cookies are actually nut-free.

MAKES 8

PREPARATION + COOKING
10 + 15 minutes

STORAGE
Store in an airtight container for up to 1 week.

SERVE THIS WITH...
plain yogurt

OMEGA-3 SOURCES
Canola oil, hemp seeds, hemp oil

NUTRITION FACTS PER PORTION
1g. vegetarian omega-3
170 calories
9g. fat
1.3g. saturated fat

1½ tsp. canola oil
½ cup hemp seeds
heaping ⅔ cup wholewheat
    pastry flour
heaping ⅔ cup all-purpose
    flour

1 tsp. pumpkin pie spice
pinch of salt
¼ cup olive oil spread
2 tbsp. sugar
1 tbsp. clear honey
1 tbsp. hemp oil

1 Preheat the oven to 350°F. Grease a baking sheet with the canola oil.
2 Set a frying pan over medium heat and toast the hemp seeds 2 minutes, then grind them in a mortar and pestle.
3 Put the flours, spice, and salt in a large bowl. Rub in the olive oil spread until the mixture resembles breadcrumbs.
4 Stir in the ground hemp seeds, sugar, honey, and hemp oil. Shape into 8 balls and place on the baking sheet.
5 Flatten the cookies using the back of a fork so that they form neat rounds. Bake 10 to 12 minutes until golden.

walnut shortbread

A teatime favorite, made even better by the addition of omega-3 rich walnuts.

1 tbsp. canola oil
½ cup wholemeal pastry flour
heaping ⅔ cup all-purpose
    flour, plus extra for rolling
¼ cup ground flax seed
¼ cup oats
1 tsp. baking powder

¼ tsp. salt
heaping ¼ cup sugar
½ cup (1 stick) butter
heaping ⅔ cup walnuts,
    chopped
1 tbsp. milk
1 tbsp. sugar, for sprinkling

1 Preheat the oven to 350°F. Grease a large baking sheet with the canola oil.

2 Sift together the two flours and ground flax seed. Add the remaining bran back into the bowl. Mix in the oats, baking powder, salt, and sugar.

3 Using your fingers, rub in the butter until the mixture resembles breadcrumbs. Add the walnuts and milk to form a dough. Gently knead on a floured surface, then roll out the dough to ¼in. thick.

4 Use a pastry cutter to cut out as many rounds as you can and put them on the baking sheet. Brush with the milk, sprinkle with the sugar, and bake 10 to 15 minutes until golden.

MAKES 10

PREPARATION + COOKING
15 + 15 minutes

STORAGE
Store in an airtight container for up to a week.

SERVE THIS WITH…
stewed fruit
ice cream

OMEGA-3 SOURCES
Canola oil, walnuts, ground flax seed

NUTRITION FACTS PER PORTION
1.4g. vegetarian omega-3
263 calories
17g. fat
6.2g. saturated fat

050

chocolate chip cookies

OMEGA-3 SOURCES
Canola oil, ground flax seed

NUTRITION FACTS PER PORTION
1.2g. vegetarian omega-3
210 calories
10g. fat
3.2g. saturated fat

These delicious soft-style cookies have a secret healthy side. Ground flax seeds are rich in nutrients such as vitamin B-1, magnesium, lignans, and vegetarian omega-3. The ground flax seed and canola oil are also great for your heart because they promote good cholesterol levels. A perfect excuse to treat yourself to another cookie.

2 tbsp. canola oil
¼ cup olive oil spread
heaped ⅓ cup unrefined sugar
1 cup all-purpose flour
1 egg, beaten

¼ cup ground flax seed
½ tsp. baking powder
½ tsp. vanilla extract
3½oz. chocolate chunks
2 tbsp. milk

MAKES 8

PREPARATION + COOKING
10 + 15 minutes

STORAGE
Store in an airtight container
for up to 2 weeks

SERVE THIS WITH...
a glass of milk

1 Preheat the oven to 350°F. Grease an 8in. baking sheet with the canola oil.

2 In a bowl, using a wooden spoon, beat the olive oil spread and sugar together until creamy. Sift the flour into the mixing bowl and add the egg. Mix well.

3 Stir in the ground flax seed, baking powder, vanilla extract, and chocolate chunks.

4 Gradually add the milk until the mixture is soft and spoonable. Spoon 8 balls onto the baking sheet and gently flatten them into rounds. They will spread out as they bake, so space them a little apart.

5 Bake the cookies 15 minutes. Remove from the oven and let cool slightly, then transfer them to cooling rack.

For a gluten-free
alternative, try
using buckwheat
flour.

051

Ⓥ ⓐ Ⓞ ⓓ ⓔ ⓕ

gingerbread cookies

MAKES 12

PREPARATION + COOKING
20 + 7 minutes

STORAGE
Store in an airtight container
for up to 2 weeks.

SERVE THIS WITH...
a glass of milk

OMEGA-3 SOURCES
Canola oil, ground flax seed,
hemp oil

NUTRITION FACTS PER PORTION
1.7g. vegetarian omega-3
130 calories
6g. fat
0.7g. saturated fat

Get the kids to help make these cookies—they
can shape them into men, animals, stars…

1 tbsp. canola oil	2 tbsp. hemp oil
1 cup plus 2 tbsp. self-rising flour	2 tbsp. light corn syrup
½ cup ground flax seed	¼ cup dark soft brown sugar
1 tsp. ground ginger	1 egg, beaten
	white icing, to decorate

1 Preheat the oven to 325°F. Grease 2 large baking sheets
with the canola oil.
2 Sift the flour, ground flax seed, and ginger into a
bowl, adding back the flax seed bran. Add the remaining
ingredients, reserving half the egg, and bring together to
form a dough. Knead briefly, then set aside 5 minutes.
3 Roll the dough to about ½in. thick and cut out the
cookies. Lay on the baking sheet, brush with egg and
bake 5 to 7 minutes until brown. Remove from the oven
and, when cool, pipe the icing onto the cookies and serve.

Ⓥ ⬤ Ⓞ ⬤ ⬤ ⬤ ⬤

frosted cupcakes

These are so quick and easy to make. Children love to help decorate them, too.

1/3 cup unrefined sugar
6 tbsp. olive oil spread
1 tbsp. flax seed oil
1 egg, beaten
1 cup self-rising flour
1/4 cup ground flax seed
1 tsp. baking powder

1 tsp. vanilla extract
1 tbsp. milk
1/4 cup chocolate chips
2/3 cup powdered sugar, sifted
decorations, such as chocolate
    chips or mini marshmallows

1 Preheat the oven to 400°F. Place 8 paper baking cups in a muffin pan.
2 Mix the sugar, olive oil spread, and oil together in a mixing bowl. Add the egg and sift in the flour, ground flax seed, and baking powder. Beat to form a smooth mixture, gradually adding the vanilla extract and enough of the milk to bring the mixture to a dropping consistency—you may not need it all. Stir in the chocolate chips.
3 Pour the mixture into the cupcake pan and bake 15 to 20 minutes until golden. Remove from the oven, turn out onto a rack, and let cool.
4 Mix the powdered sugar with 1 tbsp. water to make a smooth frosting. Frost and decorate the cakes, then serve.

MAKES 8

PREPARATION + COOKING
15 + 20 minutes

STORAGE
Store for up to 5 days in an airtight container or freeze, un-iced, for up to 1 month.

SERVE THIS WITH...
a fruit smoothie

OMEGA-3 SOURCES
Flax seed oil, ground flax seed

NUTRITION FACTS PER PORTION
1.9g. vegetarian omega-3
230 calories
10g. fat
1.6g. saturated fat

coffee & walnut cake

This moist cake is a delicious way to boost your daily omega-3 intake.

SERVES 12

PREPARATION + COOKING
10 + 45 minutes

STORAGE
Keep the iced cake in an airtight container for 1 week. Un-iced, it can be frozen for 1 month.

SERVE THIS WITH...
freshly brewed coffee

OMEGA-3 SOURCES
Walnuts, ground flax seed

NUTRITION FACTS PER PORTION
2.4g. vegetarian omega-3
429 calories
30g. fat
13g. saturated fat

²/₃ cup walnut halves
¾ cup (1½ sticks) butter
heaped ¾ cup unrefined sugar
3 eggs, beaten
1¹/₃ cups self-rising flour
½ cup ground flax seed
1 tsp. baking powder

2 tbsp. instant coffee dissolved in 2 tbsp. hot water
Icing:
½ cup (1 stick) butter
1²/₃ cups powdered sugar
1 tbsp. instant coffee dissolved in 1 tbsp. hot water

1 Preheat the oven to 325°F. Toast the nuts in the oven 8 minutes. Set 10 aside and chop the rest. Grease two 8in. cake pans and line them with baking parchment.
2 Mix the butter and sugar, then beat in the eggs. Sift in the flour, flax seed, and baking powder. Fold in the coffee and chopped walnuts, using a metal spoon. Spoon the batter into the cake pans and bake 30 minutes. Turn onto a cake rack and allow to cool.
3 For the frosting, beat together the butter and powdered sugar until smooth, then add the coffee. Add a little water, if necessary, to get a spreading consistency. Spread a third of the frosting over each cake. Set one layer on top of the other and spread the rest of the frosting around the sides. Decorate with the reserved walnut halves.

Ⓥ Ⓖ Ⓞ Ⓞ Ⓖ Ⓑ

date & walnut loaf

Juicy dates are not only delicious but also rich in iron, calcium, magnesium, and copper—all essential for a healthy nervous system.

1 tsp. canola oil
heaping ¾ cup dark brown
    sugar
¾ cup strong black tea
1 tbsp. molasses
1 tbsp. honey
¼ cup hemp oil
1¼ cups finely chopped dried
    pitted dates
½ cup raisins
⅔ cup walnuts
2½ cups all-purpose flour
1½ tsp. baking powder
2 large eggs, beaten
1 tbsp. lemon juice
1 tsp. vanilla extract

SERVES 10

PREPARATION + COOKING
20 minutes + 1 hour 10 minutes

STORAGE
This can be kept in an airtight container for up to 2 weeks or in the freezer for 1 month.

SERVE THIS WITH...
cream cheese

OMEGA-3 SOURCES
Canola oil, hemp oil, walnuts

NUTRITION FACTS PER PORTION
1.8g. vegetarian omega-3
360 calories
12g. fat
1.4g. saturated fat

1 Preheat the oven to 350°F. Grease a 1lb. loaf pan with the canola oil and line with baking parchment.
2 Put the sugar, tea, molasses, honey, and hemp oil in a saucepan and heat gently, stirring occasionally until the sugar dissolves. Add the dates, raisins, and walnuts. Simmer gently 5 minutes, then set aside to cool.
3 Sift the flour and baking powder into a mixing bowl. Stir the eggs, lemon juice, and vanilla extract into the fruit mixture, then fold the fruit mixture into the flour and mix thoroughly. Spoon into the loaf pan and bake 1 hour, or until a skewer inserted into the loaf comes out clean.
4 Turn out onto a cake rack and allow to cool, then serve.

DINNERS

Ideas for omega-3 rich dinners are essential to family life since it's an opportunity to make sure that everyone eats at least some of these essential fats every day. For midweek meals, Seafood Lasagne is a new twist on an old classic, or if you prefer something spicy, omega-3 packed walnuts and soybeans make Moroccan Tagine a simple yet mouthwatering way to boost your family's health. If you're expecting friends for dinner, the visual drama of Moules Marinière always adds to the entertainment of the evening. Delicious Crab Cakes can be prepared in advance and cooked in eight minutes flat. And for those nights when you simply want something quickly, a healthy Spicy Crab Linguine can be whipped up in ten speedy minutes. Perfect!

SERVES 4

PREPARATION + COOKING
20 + 35 minutes

STORAGE
Refrigerate for up to 5 days or
freeze for up to 3 months.

SERVE THIS WITH...
steamed rice
mango chutney

OMEGA-3 SOURCES
Hemp seeds, walnuts,
ground flax seed

NUTRITION FACTS PER PORTION
6g. vegetarian omega-3
470 calories
39g. fat
11g. saturated fat

curried hemp & nut roast

A vegetarian classic, this delicious loaf is full of flavor and is brimming with omega-3.

1 cup hemp seeds	2 tbsp. tomato paste
1 small onion, chopped	2 garlic cloves, crushed
1½ cups chopped mushrooms	½ tsp. cumin
heaping ½ cup grated zucchini	½ tsp. cayenne pepper
heaping ½ cup grated carrot	½ tsp. ground coriander
⅔ cup walnut pieces	1 egg
¼ cup creamed coconut	salt
½ cup ground flax seed	freshly ground black pepper

1 Preheat the oven to 375°F. Grease a 1lb. loaf pan.

2 Dry-fry the hemp seeds in a skillet for a couple of minutes and then crush in a mortar and pestle.

3 Mix together all the ingredients in a large bowl and season with salt and pepper. Shape the mixture into the loaf pan and bake 30 to 35 minutes until lightly browned. Serve immediately.

Ⓥ ⊙ Ⓞ ⊘ ⊛ ▷

japanese tofu stir-fry

Thickly sliced tofu steaks are transformed by marinating them in Japanese teriyaki sauce.

1lb. 2oz. tofu, cut into 4 slices
1 tbsp. canola oil
2 garlic cloves, chopped
4 mushrooms, sliced
1 zucchini, sliced
1 red bell pepper, sliced
1 green bell pepper, sliced
½ red onion, sliced
7oz. bok choy, sliced
2 tsp. cornstarch

2 tbsp. hemp oil
7oz. fresh egg noodles
1 tbsp. flax seeds
2 scallions, sliced

Teriyaki Sauce:
½ cup soy sauce
½ cup mirin
½ cup sake
1 tbsp. sugar

1 Gently heat the teriyaki sauce ingredients in a skillet. Add the tofu and cook very gently 10 to 15 minutes.
2 Transfer the tofu steaks to a baking sheet, reserving the sauce. Broil the tofu 5 to 10 minutes, turning once.
3 Heat the canola oil in another skillet and stir-fry the garlic and vegetables 3 minutes.
4 Blend the cornstarch and hemp oil, add the reserved sauce, and return it to the pan. Heat gently until thick.
5 Cook the noodles according to the packet instructions. Toast the flax seeds under the broiler. Slice the tofu into strips and mix with the vegetables and sauce. Serve on the noodles, sprinkled with the flax seeds and scallions.

SERVES 4

PREPARATION + COOKING
25 + 35 minutes

STORAGE
This dish is not suitable for the refrigerator or freezer.

SERVE THIS WITH...
Hot Chocolate Pears
(see page 127)

OMEGA-3 SOURCES
Tofu, canola oil, hemp oil, flax seeds

NUTRITION FACTS PER PORTION
4g. vegetarian omega-3
610 calories
27g. fat
4g. saturated fat

bean & vegetable chili

A classic, versatile chili that can be served on rice, in tacos, or as enchiladas.

SERVES 4

PREPARATION + COOKING
10 + 30 minutes

STORAGE
This will keep in the refrigerator for up to 3 days or in the freezer for 3 months.

SERVE THIS WITH...
flour tortillas
guacamole
sour cream
grated cheddar cheese

OMEGA-3 SOURCES
Canola oil, soybeans

NUTRITION FACTS PER PORTION
1.1g. vegetarian omega-3
405 calories
25g. fat
2.5g. saturated fat

2 tbsp. canola oil
1 small red onion, finely sliced
2 garlic cloves, crushed
1 chili, chopped
1 orange bell pepper, diced
1 small zucchini, diced
1½ cups diced mushrooms
28oz. canned chopped tomatoes

½ cup chopped sun-dried tomatoes
1 tbsp. tomato paste
1 vegetable bouillon cube
1½ cups canned soybeans
¾ cup canned kidney beans
salt
freshly ground black pepper

1 Heat the oil in a large pan and add the onion, garlic, and chili. Cook 3 to 5 minutes, then add the pepper and zucchini and cook a further 2 to 3 minutes. Finally, add the mushrooms and cook another 3 minutes until soft.
2 Add the canned and sun-dried tomatoes, tomato paste, bouillon, beans, and 1¾ cups hot water. Simmer 20 minutes. Season with salt and pepper to taste and serve.

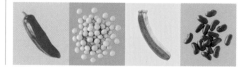

Ⓥ 🍃 🌾 🍀 🍂 🍃

parmesan peppers with balsamic tofu

The balsamic vinegar adds a sweetness that perfectly complements the roasted peppers.

2 tbsp. hemp oil
2 tbsp. balsamic vinegar
2 tbsp. roughly chopped basil
9oz. tofu, roughly chopped
4 bell peppers, halved and
    deseeded
1 tbsp. canola oil
1½ cups finely chopped
    mushrooms

⅓ cup finely chopped
    sun-dried tomatoes
salt
freshly ground black pepper

Parmesan Crust:
½ cup hemp seeds
⅔ cup grated Parmesan cheese
½ cup fresh breadcrumbs

SERVES 4

PREPARATION + COOKING
15 + 30 minutes

STORAGE
This will keep in the refrigerator for up to 3 days.

SERVE THIS WITH...
Mixed Bean Salad (see page 46)
jacket potato

OMEGA-3 SOURCES
Hemp oil, tofu, canola oil, hemp seeds

NUTRITION FACTS PER PORTION
2.8g. vegetarian omega-3
330 calories
23g. fat
5g. saturated fat

1 Preheat the oven to 350°F. Combine the hemp oil, vinegar, and basil in a bowl. Add the tofu.

2 Brush the peppers with the canola oil. Set on a baking sheet and bake 10 to 15 minutes until softened.

3 Meanwhile, dry-fry the hemp seeds 2 to 3 minutes and then crush them using a mortar and pestle. Add the Parmesan and breadcrumbs.

4 Add the mushrooms and tomatoes to the tofu, season, and spoon into the cooked peppers. Top with the Parmesan crust and bake 15 minutes until browned.

Ⓥ ⬤ ⬤ ⬤ ⬤

soybean & tofu laksa

Laksa is a fragrant Malaysian curry with noodles and crisp vegetables.

SERVES 4

PREPARATION + COOKING
10 + 20 minutes

STORAGE
This will keep in the refrigerator for 3 days or in the freezer for up to 3 months.

SERVE THIS WITH...
Mango and Banana Smoothie (see page 24)

OMEGA-3 SOURCES
Canola oil, tofu, soybeans

NUTRITION FACTS PER PORTION
1.5g. vegetarian omega-3
650 calories
37g. fat
2.4g. saturated fat

1 tbsp. canola oil
2 small red chilies, sliced
6 scallions, finely chopped
2 red bell peppers, finely chopped
¼ cup vegetarian red Thai curry paste
1lb. 2oz. tofu, diced
1 heaping cup canned soybeans
¼ cup light soy sauce
3½ cups reduced-fat coconut milk
2½ cups boiling water
6oz. rice noodles
handful cilantro, roughly chopped, plus a few sprigs, to serve
1 tomato, finely chopped

1 Heat the canola oil in a pan set over medium heat. Add the chili, four of the scallions, and the peppers and cook about 5 minutes until softened.

2 Add the curry paste and fry 2 minutes, then add the tofu and fry a further 2 minutes, stirring gently.

3 Add the soybeans, soy sauce, coconut milk, and 2½ cups water, bring to a boil, then turn the heat down and simmer the curry about 5 minutes.

4 Add the noodles and cilantro and simmer 2 minutes. Serve sprinkled with the remaining scallions, the chopped tomato, and the reserved cilantro sprigs.

(V) (43)

thai soybean cakes with bell pepper sauce

Gluten-free gram flour, made from chick peas, is traditional to Asian cooking. All-purpose flour also works in this recipe.

2¼ cups canned soybeans
1 large onion, roughly chopped
large handful cilantro
2 tsp. vegetarian Thai curry
   paste
juice and zest of 1 lime
½ cup gram flour
2 tbsp. canola oil

4 lime slices
salt
freshly ground black pepper

Red Pepper Sauce:
2 red bell peppers, chopped
¼ cup apple juice
1 tbsp. cider/wine vinegar
2 dried red chilies, chopped

1 Simmer all the red pepper sauce ingredients in a pan over low heat until the peppers are softened. Transfer to a blender and blend to make a thin sauce. Season to taste with salt and pepper.

2 Blend the soybeans, onion, cilantro, Thai curry paste, and lime in a food processor for 30 seconds.

3 Shape the soybean mixture into 4 patties. Put the flour in a shallow bowl and carefully coat the bean cakes.

4 Heat the oil in a pan and fry the cakes 5 minutes, turning once. Serve hot with the pepper sauce and lime slices.

SERVES 4

PREPARATION + COOKING
20 + 10 minutes

STORAGE
Keep the separated cakes and sauce in the refrigerator for up to 3 days or in the freezer for up to 3 months

SERVE THIS WITH...
Indonesian Spicy Rice
 (see page 122)

OMEGA-3 SOURCES
Soybeans, canola oil

NUTRITION FACTS PER PORTION
1.3g. vegetarian omega-3
350 calories
19g. fat
1.9g. saturated fat

*moroccan tagine

OMEGA-3 SOURCES
Canola oil, soybeans, walnuts, walnut oil

NUTRITION FACTS PER PORTION
1.8g. vegetarian omega-3
695 calories
31g. fat
2.9g. saturated fat

This spicy tagine is served with a delicious walnut couscous. A true superfood, walnuts are not only the richest form of vegetarian omega-3, but also contain protein, healthy oils, vitamins, and minerals, which may help lower blood cholesterol levels.

1 tsp. cumin seeds
½ tsp. mild cayenne pepper
½ tsp. ground coriander
½ tsp. ground allspice
½ tsp. paprika
1 tbsp. canola oil
1 red onion, chopped
2 garlic cloves, crushed
2 sweet potatoes, peeled and
   chopped into bite-size dice
1 green bell pepper, chopped

5 cups vegetable stock
15oz. canned soybeans
½ cup dried apricots
¼ cup raisins
2 tbsp. chopped cilantro

Walnut Couscous:
2¼ cups couscous
scant ½ cup walnuts
2 tbsp. walnut oil

SERVES 4

PREPARATION + COOKING
15 + 40 minutes

STORAGE
The tagine can be stored in the refrigerator for 3 to 4 days or in the freezer for 1 month. The couscous is best prepared fresh.

1 Dry-fry the spices 2 to 3 minutes in a casserole dish over low heat. Add the canola oil, onion, garlic, and vegetables and cook, stirring, 5 minutes until softened.
2 Add the stock to the pan along with the beans, apricots, and raisins. Cover with a lid and simmer 40 minutes.
3 In a bowl, pour 3½ cups hot water over the couscous and let soak 5 minutes. Meanwhile, toast the walnuts under the broiler. Fluff the couscous, using a fork, and gently mix in the walnut oil and walnuts. Serve with the tagine, sprinkled with cilantro.

SERVE THIS WITH...
a dollop of sour cream

Try to use organic unsulfured dried apricots when you make this dish.

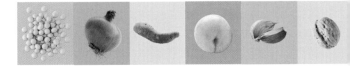

062

moules marinière

Rich in omega-3, mussels are surprisingly quick to cook—a truly healthy fast food.

SERVES 4

PREPARATION + COOKING
5 + 15 minutes

STORAGE
This dish is not suitable for the refrigerator or freezer.

SERVE THIS WITH...
warm crusty bread
French fries

OMEGA-3 SOURCES
Mussels

NUTRITION FACTS PER PORTION
1.8g. fish omega-3
365 calories
14g. fat
4.3g. saturated fat

1 tbsp. olive oil
2 garlic cloves, chopped
2 shallots, finely chopped
1 bouquet garni—small handful parsley, thyme and bay leaf, tied together with string

4lb. mussels, cleaned and beards removed
¹/₃ cup dry white wine
½ cup reduced fat sour cream
handful parsley, chopped

1 Make sure that all the mussels are tightly closed. Discard any that will not close when touched.
2 Gently heat the oil in a large saucepan and add the garlic, shallots, and bouquet garni. Add the mussels and wine, turn up the heat, then cover and cook 3 to 4 minutes. Shake the pan occasionally. Discard any mussels that fail to open during cooking.
3 Remove the bouquet garni, add the sour cream and parsley, and remove from the heat.
4 Serve in large bowls with lots of crusty bread.

seafood paella

This appetizing Spanish paella is a great example of healthy Mediterranean food.

1 tbsp. canola oil
1 garlic clove, crushed
1 red onion, chopped
1 red bell pepper, chopped
1 tsp. paprika
2 cups arborio rice
¼ tsp. saffron strands

2½ cups fish stock
½ cup frozen peas
4oz. raw shrimp, peeled and
    deveined
4oz. mussels
4oz. squid rings
⅓ cup white wine

1 Heat the oil in a large pan and add the garlic, onion, pepper, and paprika. Cook 2 minutes until the onion becomes translucent. Add the rice and cook another 2 minutes until the rice grains are glossy.

2 Add the saffron strands to the fish stock, then pour it into the pan and stir well. Bring to a boil, add the peas, then simmer 20 minutes until the rice starts to soften.

3 Add the seafood and white wine and simmer 5 minutes. Stir in the parsley and serve hot.

SERVES 4

PREPARATION + COOKING
5 + 25 minutes

STORAGE
This dish is not suitable for the refrigerator or freezer.

SERVE THIS WITH...
Grilled chicken thighs

OMEGA-3 SOURCES
Shrimp, mussels, squid, canola oil

NUTRITION FACTS PER PORTION
0.5g. fish omega-3
0.4g. vegetarian omega-3
470 calories
9g. fat
1.2g. saturated fat

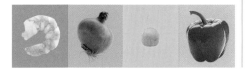

064

spicy crab linguine

The fresh cooked pasta warms the crab sauce and makes this succulent pasta dish sublime.

SERVES 4

PREPARATION + COOKING
5 + 5 minutes

STORAGE
The crab sauce can be kept in the refrigerator for 2 days.

SERVE THIS WITH...
Dressed Green Salad
  (see page 43)

OMEGA-3 SOURCES
Crab

NUTRITION FACTS PER PORTION
0.6g. fish omega-3
537 calories
18g. fat
2.1g. saturated fat

10oz. crab meat	2 scallions, chopped
juice and zest of 1 lemon	2 tsp. dried chili flakes
juice and zest of 1 lime	1 tsp. sea salt
1 garlic clove, crushed	3 tbsp. olive oil
2 tbsp. chopped parsley	1lb. 2oz. fresh linguine

1 In a bowl, mix together the crab with all the ingredients except the pasta.

2 Cook the linguine in a large pot of boiling water 5 minutes or according to the packet instructions. Drain well.

3 Toss the pasta into the crab mixture and stir it all together. Serve immediately.

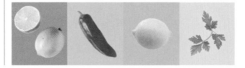

smoked salmon & parmesan tortellini

Smoked salmon is a delicious source of omega-3 fats and may help conditions such as asthma, Crohn's disease, and arthritis.

2 tbsp. olive oil
2 large shallots, finely chopped
scant 2 cups sliced mushrooms
7oz. smoked salmon, cut into
   strips

1lb. 5oz. fresh spinach &
   ricotta tortellini pasta
1 cup crème fraîche
²/₃ cup grated Parmesan cheese
24 capers

1 Gently heat the oil in a skillet, add the shallots, and cook 5 minutes. Add the mushrooms and salmon and cook 2 to 3 minutes until the salmon becomes opaque.

2 Meanwhile, cook the pasta in boiling water 2 minutes. Drain and stir into the salmon along with the crème fraîche and Parmesan. Sprinkle with the capers and serve.

SERVES 4

PREPARATION + COOKING
5 + 10 minutes

STORAGE
This is not suitable for the refrigerator or freezer.

SERVE THIS WITH...
broccoli
asparagus

OMEGA-3 SOURCES
Salmon

NUTRITION FACTS PER PORTION
0.9g. fish omega-3
529 calories
23g. fat
13g. saturated fat

990

😊 😊 💧 🍋 🌿

crab cakes

This supper recipe could also make smaller
crab cakes for a tasty appetizer or light meal.

1lb. 1oz. canned white crab
  meat, drained, and flaked
6oz. canned brown crab meat,
  drained
6 scallions, finely chopped
large handful cilantro, finely
  chopped

juice of 2 limes
2 tsp. dried chili flakes
2 garlic cloves, crushed
½ cup flour
2 eggs, beaten
1 cup fresh breadcrumbs
¼ cup canola oil

1 Mix the white and brown crab meat together in a mixing
bowl. Stir in the scallions, cilantro, lime juice, chili flakes,
and garlic. Set aside to marinate 15 minutes.
2 Divide the mixture into quarters and, using your hands,
shape it into 8 patties. Coat with flour, dip in the egg, and
then in the breadcrumbs.
3 Heat the oil in a skillet over medium heat and fry the
crab cakes 2 minutes on each side. You may need to do
this in batches. Serve immediately.

sweet chili, squid & shrimp stir-fry

Squid is a good omega-3 source and has the added benefit of being very swift to cook.

1½ cups sweet chili sauce
¾ cup soy sauce
1lb. 12oz. squid, cleaned, quill removed, and sliced
1lb. 12oz. raw shrimp, peeled and deveined
½ cup canola oil

1lb. bok choy, finely sliced
2 red bell peppers, finely sliced
12 scallions, finely sliced
8oz. canned whole baby corn, sliced
1½ cups sliced broccoli florets
8oz. fresh egg noodles

1 Put the chili and soy sauces in a dish. Stir in the squid and marinate in the refrigerator at least 4 hours.
2 When ready to cook, add the shrimp to the marinade.
3 Heat the oil in a wok and add the vegetables. Stir-fry 2 to 3 minutes. Using a slotted spoon, add the squid and shrimp to the wok and stir-fry 2 minutes.
4 Add the noodles and the marinade to the wok and stir-fry a further 2 minutes. Serve immediately.

SERVES 4

PREPARATION + COOKING
5 + 5 minutes + marinating

STORAGE
Keep the marinated squid in the refrigerator for up to 2 days.

SERVE THIS WITH...
bean sprouts
shrimp crackers

OMEGA-3 SOURCES
Squid, shrimp, canola oil

NUTRITION FACTS PER PORTION
1g. fish omega-3
1g. vegetarian omega-3
610 calories
19g. fat
1.7g. saturated fat

⚹ ⚹ ○ ⊘ ⚘

shrimp wrapped in sea bass fillets

This is a great light supper dish and is even impressive enough to serve at a dinner party.

SERVES 4

PREPARATION + COOKING
10 + 20 minutes

STORAGE
This is not suitable for the refrigerator or freezer.

SERVE THIS WITH...
Apple & Peach Crumble
(see page 128)

OMEGA-3 SOURCES
Canola oil, sea bass, shrimp

NUTRITION FACTS PER PORTION
1.0g. fish omega-3
0.5g. vegetarian omega-3
444 calories
19g. fat
2.5g. saturated fat

1 tbsp. canola oil
2 red bell peppers, sliced
12 long slices of zucchini
2 garlic cloves, chopped
4 x 5½oz. sea bass fillets
8 raw jumbo shrimp, peeled and deveined

2 tbsp. olive oil
10½oz. fresh egg tagliatelle
2 tsp. chopped parsley
salt
freshly ground black pepper

1 Preheat the oven to 350°F. Warm the canola oil in a baking pan in the oven. Add the vegetables and garlic. Bake 10 minutes, remove from the oven and keep warm.
2 Meanwhile, season the fillets with salt and pepper, then wrap each one, skin-side out, around 2 shrimp, leaving the heads poking out. Secure using toothpicks. Brush with half the olive oil, set on a baking sheet, and roast 10 minutes.
3 Cook the tagliatelle in boiling water 2 minutes, then drain. Toss in the rest of the olive oil, the vegetables, parsley, and seasoning. Serve the sea bass, shrimp, and pasta drizzled with the cooking juices.

fish fingers

These are great for kids, plus they can have a go at the mashing, shaping, and dipping!

8oz. potatoes, peeled
1 tbsp. olive oil spread
²/₃ cup milk, warmed
5½oz. salmon

9oz. cod or pollock
3 tbsp. all-purpose flour
1 egg, beaten
1 cup cornflakes, crushed

1 Boil the potatoes 15 minutes in a pan of water, until tender. Drain the potatoes and mash them with the olive oil spread and 2 tablespoons of the milk.
2 Put the fish in a small saucepan and pour in the remaining milk. Simmer over low heat 5 minutes until the fish is cooked through. Drain and flake the fish, then mix it into the mashed potato, using a fork.
3 Shape into 12 finger shapes and chill 15 minutes.
4 Preheat the broiler. Roll the fish fingers in the flour, then the egg, and finally the cornflakes. Broil the fish fingers for 10 minutes or until golden and serve immediately.

SERVES 4

PREPARATION + COOKING
20 + 30 minutes + chilling

STORAGE
This will keep in the refrigerator for 24 hours. Freeze them for up to 3 months.

SERVE THIS WITH...
baked beans

OMEGA-3 SOURCES
Salmon, cod

NUTRITION FACTS PER PORTION
0.8g. fish omega-3
300 calories
8g. fat
1.3g. saturated fat

seafood & lentil stew

This hearty Mediterranean stew has a little spicy heat from the chilies.

SERVES 4

PREPARATION + COOKING
5 + 20 minutes

STORAGE
This can be kept in the refrigerator for 2 days.

SERVE THIS WITH...
cheese topped garlic bread

OMEGA-3 SOURCES
Canola oil, cod, shrimp, mussels, squid

NUTRITION FACTS PER PORTION
0.7g. fish omega-3
0.4g. vegetarian omega-3
280 calories
7g. fat
0.8g. saturated fat

1 tbsp. canola oil
1 large onion, diced
2 garlic cloves, crushed
1 tsp. chili flakes
1 tsp. smoked paprika
5½oz. cod, cut into chunks
28oz. canned chopped
   tomatoes

2½ cups fish stock
⅓ cup dried red lentils
8oz. raw shrimp, peeled and
   deveined
4oz. mussels
4oz. squid
2 tbsp. brandy

1 Heat the oil in a large pan, add the onion and garlic, and fry gently 3 to 4 minutes until softened. Add the chili flakes and paprika and stir well.

2 Add the cod to the pan, coating it well in the spices. Add the tomatoes and stock and bring to a simmer. Add the lentils and simmer 10 minutes until the lentils soften.

3 Add the seafood and brandy and heat through a further 10 minutes. Serve hot.

thai shrimp curry

A classic red Thai curry. The aromatic herbs and spices make this a treat for the senses.

1½ cups jasmine rice
1 tbsp. canola oil
1 large onion, chopped
1 red bell pepper, chopped
1 lemongrass stalk, finely
    chopped
2 garlic cloves, crushed
1 tsp. ground ginger
1 tsp. chili flakes

2 tomatoes, chopped
1 fish bouillon cube
juice of ½ lime
2 kaffir lime leaves
14oz. canned reduced-fat
    coconut milk
1lb. 2oz. cooked, peeled jumbo
    shrimp
2 tbsp. chopped cilantro

1 Boil the rice 12 to 15 minutes or according to the packet instructions. Meanwhile, heat the oil in a skillet and gently fry the onion, pepper, lemongrass, garlic, ginger, and chili flakes 5 minutes until soft.

2 Add the tomatoes, fish bouillon, lime juice, kaffir lime leaves, and coconut milk and simmer 5 minutes. Remove the kaffir lime leaves and remove from the heat.

3 In a blender, or using a hand blender, blend the mixture 1 to 2 minutes to make a pale red sauce.

4 Return the sauce to the pan and add the shrimp. Bring gently to a simmer 5 minutes. Stir in the cilantro and serve immediately with the jasmine rice.

SERVES 4

PREPARATION + COOKING
5 + 20 minutes

STORAGE
This can be kept for 2 days in the refrigerator.

SERVE THIS WITH...
Five Spice Tofu Salad
  (see page 44)

OMEGA-3 SOURCES
Canola oil, jumbo shrimp

NUTRITION FACTS PER PORTION
0.6g. fish omega-3
0.4g. vegetarian omega-3
589 calories
19g. fat
0.7g. saturated fat

072

baked salmon parcels

This simple dish is baked in a foil parcel, which keeps in all the luscious flavors and moisture.

SERVES 4

PREPARATION + COOKING
35 + 25 minutes

STORAGE
The marinated salmon will keep for 24 hours in the refrigerator. Once cooked it can be chilled for just 2 days.

SERVE THIS WITH...
boiled new potatoes
green beans

OMEGA-3 SOURCES
Salmon, canola oil

NUTRITION FACTS PER PORTION
2.3g. fish omega-3
0.5g. vegetarian omega-3
331 calories
22g. fat
3.5g. saturated fat

4 x 4½oz. salmon steaks
¼ cup balsamic vinegar
2 tbsp. olive oil
1 tsp. brown sugar

½ red onion, finely chopped
1 tbsp. canola oil
salt
freshly ground black pepper

1 Place the salmon in a dish. Whisk together the balsamic vinegar, olive oil, sugar, and seasoning. Stir in the onion and pour this over the fish. Cover and let marinate in the refrigerator at least 30 minutes or ideally up to 4 hours.
2 Preheat the oven to 350°F. Lay out four 12in. squares of aluminum foil.
3 Brush the salmon with the canola oil, then lay each one on a piece of foil and fold it into a loose bundle.
4 Place the bundles on a baking sheet. Bake 20 minutes until the salmon is just cooked in the middle. Unwrap and serve drizzled with the cooking juices.

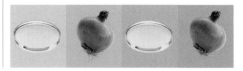

salmon & spinach risotto

This traditional-style risotto will boost your body's iron levels along with your omega-3.

1lb. 2oz. salmon fillets
1 onion, finely chopped
1 tbsp. canola oil
2 garlic cloves, crushed
2 cups arborio rice
4⅓ cups fish stock

scant 1 cup white wine
2 large handfuls baby spinach
1¾ cups hot water
⅓ cup grated Parmesan cheese
salt
freshly ground black pepper

1 Partly cook the salmon fillets in a suitable covered dish in the microwave 3 minutes on full power; or poach in 2 tablespoons of water in a pan 5 minutes until the salmon is pink in the middle. Set aside.

2 Gently fry the onion in the canola oil 3 to 4 minutes. Add the garlic and rice and fry a further 2 minutes.

3 Add the stock and wine to the rice, bring to a boil, and simmer gently 10 minutes, stirring occasionally.

4 Remove the skin and roughly flake the salmon. Add this, along with the spinach, to the rice. Add about 1¾ cups hot water to moisten the dish. Season with salt and pepper. Simmer 2 to 3 minutes. Serve immediately, sprinkled with the grated Parmesan cheese.

SERVES 4

PREPARATION + COOKING
10 + 20 minutes

STORAGE
This will keep in the refrigerator for 3 days or in the freezer for up to 1 month.

SERVE THIS WITH...
crisp salad greens
cherry tomatoes

OMEGA-3 SOURCES
Salmon, canola oil, spinach

NUTRITION FACTS PER PORTION
2.3g. fish omega-3
0.5g. vegetarian omega-3
680 calories
20g. fat
4g. saturated fat

PREPARATION + COOKING
15 + 35 minutes

STORAGE
This dish is not suitable for the refrigerator or freezer.

SERVE THIS WITH...
Walnut Couscous
(see page 94)

OMEGA-3 SOURCES
Sardines

NUTRITION FACTS PER PORTION
1.7g. fish omega-3
324 calories
27g. fat
3g. saturated fat

moroccan sardines

Butterfly fillets mean that the two halves of the sardine fillet are still joined down the back.

2 tomatoes, finely chopped
²/₃ cup apricots, finely chopped
¼ cup pitted black olives, finely chopped
2 garlic cloves, crushed
1 tsp. cayenne pepper

1 tsp. smoked paprika
4 tsp. lemon juice
large pinch of salt
8 fresh sardine fillets, descaled and butterflied
½ cup white wine

1 Preheat the oven to 350°F. Mix the tomatoes, apricots, and olives together with the garlic, chili, paprika, lemon juice, and salt.
2 Line 2 baking sheets with foil and lay 4 fillets on each. Stuff the sardines with the filling and secure with toothpicks. Pour over the wine, then wrap in the foil.
3 Bake 30 minutes, then unwrap and put under a preheated broiler 5 minutes to crisp up the skins. Serve immediately.

easy salmon & pesto quiche

A little pesto goes a long way and transforms this quiche from good to excellent.

8 sheets phyllo dough
2 tbsp. canola oil
12¾oz. canned salmon fillet
8oz. mascarpone cheese
4 eggs

2 tbsp. ready-made pesto
⅓ cup grated Parmesan cheese
salt
freshly ground black pepper

1 Preheat the oven to 350°F. Brush the phyllo sheets with the canola oil and layer them in an 8in. tart pan. Take care to completely cover the bottom and sides of the pan.
2 Mix the salmon, mascarpone, eggs, and pesto together in a bowl, season with salt and pepper, and then pour into the tart pan.
3 Bake 15 minutes until nearly set, then sprinkle the grated Parmesan cheese on top. Return it to the oven and bake a further 5 to 10 minutes until golden brown. Serve either warm or cold.

SERVES 6

PREPARATION + COOKING
10 + 25 minutes

STORAGE
This will keep in the refrigerator for 3 days or frozen for up to 3 months.

SERVE THIS WITH...
Watercress, Walnut, Pear & Roquefort Salad (see page 42)

OMEGA-3 SOURCES
Canola oil, salmon

NUTRITION FACTS PER PORTION
0.8g. fish omega-3
0.5g. vegetarian omega-3
450 calories
33g. fat
15g. saturated fat

OMEGA-3 SOURCES
Canola oil, shrimp,
mussels, squid

NUTRITION FACTS PER PORTION
0.6g. fish omega-3
0.5g. vegetarian omega-3
495 calories
16g. fat
3.2g. saturated fat

*seafood lasagne

Straight from the Mediterranean, where fresh fish and seafood feature regularly at the evening meal, this stunning lasagne makes the most of scrumptious shrimp, mussels, and squid. Rich in essential omega-3 fats and key vitamins and minerals, it makes a healthy, hearty, filling dish.

1 tbsp. canola oil
1 large onion, roughly chopped
2 garlic cloves, crushed
1 zucchini, chopped
1¾ cups tomato puree
¼ cup fish stock
1lb. 2oz. frozen seafood
1¼ cups milk
1 bay leaf

5 black peppercorns
2 tbsp. olive oil spread
1 level tbsp. all-purpose flour
8 lasagne sheets
2oz. cheddar cheese, grated
1oz. Gruyère cheese, grated
salt
freshly ground black pepper

SERVES 4

PREPARATION + COOKING
15 + 40 minutes

STORAGE
Store in the refrigerator
overnight and eat the following
day. Not suitable for freezing.

1 Preheat the oven to 400°F. Heat the oil and fry the onion and garlic 2 minutes. Add the zucchini, tomato puree, stock, salt and pepper. Simmer 3 minutes, then add the seafood. Let simmer while you make the white sauce.

2 Put the milk, bay leaf, and peppercorns in a bowl and heat in a microwave on high for 1 minute. Melt the olive oil spread in a pan and stir in the flour. Stirring well, strain in the milk and cook gently to form a smooth white sauce.

3 Pour one third of the seafood sauce into a baking dish and cover with 4 lasagne sheets. Repeat these 2 layers, then top with the remaining seafood sauce.

4 Pour the white sauce over the seafood and sprinkle with the cheeses. Bake 40 minutes until golden.

SERVE THIS WITH...
a green salad
garlic bread
Lemon Curd Puddings
  (see page 134)

A typical frozen
seafood mix
would include
shrimp, mussels,
and squid—an
ideal mixture.

SERVES 4

PREPARATION + COOKING
15 + 25 minutes

STORAGE
Refrigerate the cooked fish and eat within 1 day.

SERVE THIS WITH…
braised fennel
boiled new potatoes

OMEGA-3 SOURCES
Canola oil, halibut

NUTRITION FACTS PER PORTION
0.7g. fish omega-3
0.4g. vegetarian omega-3
270 calories
9g. fat
1g. saturated fat

provençal halibut

This delicious healthy dish encapsulates the Provençal ethos to eat well and live well.

1½ tsp. canola oil
1 onion, thinly sliced
2 garlic cloves, crushed
4 tomatoes, chopped
1 zucchini, sliced
1 red bell pepper, sliced
4 x 6oz. halibut fillets

¼ cup pitted black olives
4 small sprigs of rosemary
4 bay leaves
4 sprigs of thyme
¼ cup white wine
salt
freshly ground black pepper

1 Preheat the oven to 375°F. Prepare 4 large squares of aluminum foil.

2 Heat 1 teaspoon of the canola oil in a pan and gently fry the onion and garlic. Add the tomatoes, zucchini, and pepper to the pan and cook 5 minutes with the lid on.

3 Brush the foil with the remaining canola oil. Put 1 heaping tablespoon of the vegetable mixture on each piece of foil and lay a halibut fillet on top. Season with salt and pepper, top with another tablespoon of mixture, and pour the juices over the bundles. Sprinkle with the olives.

4 Lay one of each of the herb sprigs on top, pour the wine over, and fold the foil into a bundle. Place the bundles in a roasting pan and bake 25 minutes. Serve immediately.

pasta niçoise

This is a great twist on the classic Niçoise salad, using pasta instead of salad greens.

4 eggs
6oz. green beans
2 tbsp. canola oil
2 garlic cloves, crushed
4 x 5oz. tuna steaks
3 cups fusilli pasta

32 cherry tomatoes, halved
½ cup pitted black olives, halved
2 tbsp. chopped parsley
salt
freshly ground black pepper

1 Boil the eggs 10 minutes, then drain and set aside. Boil the beans 5 minutes, then drain and set aside.
2 Heat the oil in a skillet and add the garlic. Sear the tuna 5 minutes on each side. Remove from the pan and set aside. Boil the pasta 10 to 12 minutes, then drain.
3 Gently reheat the skillet, add the tomatoes, and cook 3 to 4 minutes. Add the pasta to the tomatoes and stir in the olives and beans. Season with salt and pepper.
4 Peel and quarter the hard-boiled eggs. Serve the pasta with the tuna and eggs and sprinkled with the parsley.

SERVES 4

PREPARATION + COOKING
10 + 30 minutes

STORAGE
This dish is not suitable for the refrigerator or freezer.

SERVE THIS WITH...
Dressed Green Salad
(see page 43)

OMEGA-3 SOURCES
Canola oil, tuna

NUTRITION FACTS PER PORTION
1.7g. fish omega-3
0.8g. vegetarian omega-3
650 calories
20g. fat
3g. saturated fat

079

tuna in tomato sauce

An omega-3 variation on meatballs in tomato sauce, this is always popular with children.

SERVES 4

PREPARATION + COOKING
15 + 15 minutes

STORAGE
The tuna balls can be frozen for up to 1 month.

SERVE THIS WITH…
spaghetti
Parmesan cheese

OMEGA-3 SOURCES
Tuna, canola oil

NUTRITION FACTS PER PORTION
0.8g. fish omega-3
237 calories
11g. fat
1.8g. saturated fat

9oz. fresh tuna
1 small onion, finely chopped
1 cup breadcrumbs
1 garlic clove, crushed
1 tsp. dried oregano
1 egg, beaten
12oz. tomato puree

14oz. canned chopped tomatoes
¼ cup black pitted olives
1 tbsp. canola oil
salt
freshly ground black pepper

1 Put the tuna in a shallow dish, cover with plastic wrap, and cook in the microwave on full power 2 minutes. Remove and set aside.

2 In a bowl, mix the onion together with the breadcrumbs, garlic, and oregano and season with salt and pepper.

3 Finely chop the tuna and mix it, with the egg, into the breadcrumb mixture. Chill in the refrigerator 10 minutes.

4 Shape the tuna mixture into 12 balls in the palm of your hand. Heat the oil in a large pan and brown the balls in the hot oil for a few minutes, then set aside.

5 Mix the tomato puree and tomatoes together in a pan over medium heat. Add the tuna balls and olives and simmer 10 minutes. Serve hot.

pissaladière

Anchovies and olives are the definitive flavors here—somewhere between a tart and a pizza.

1 tbsp. canola oil
2 onions, finely sliced
2 garlic cloves, crushed
7oz. ready-made puff pastry
1 tbsp all-purpose flour, for
    rolling the pastry

3 tbsp. ready-made pesto
3 tomatoes, thinly sliced
¼ cup pitted black olives
2¼oz. drained anchovy fillets

1 Preheat the oven to 400°F. Heat the oil in a saucepan and cook the onions and garlic over low heat 15 to 20 minutes until they start to caramelize and turn brown.
2 Meanwhile, roll out the puff pastry on a floured surface and line an 8 x 12in. baking sheet with baking parchment.
3 Spread the pesto over the puff pastry, evenly spoon over the onions, and cover with tomato slices and olives. Finally, arrange the anchovy fillets in a criss-cross pattern.
4 Bake 20 to 30 minutes or until the edge of the puff pastry is well risen and golden. Serve immediately.

SERVES 4

PREPARATION + COOKING
20 + 30 minutes

STORAGE
This can be stored in the refrigerator for up to 2 days.

SERVE THIS WITH...
Watercress, Walnut, Pear &
    Roquefort Salad (see page 42)

OMEGA-3 SOURCES
Canola oil, anchovies

NUTRITION FACTS PER PORTION
0.3g. fish omega-3
0.7g. vegetarian omega-3
415 calories
29g. fat
2g. saturated fat

spicy tuna burgers

These are a healthy alternative to beef burgers. They cook just as well on the barbecue, too.

SERVES 4

PREPARATION + COOKING
10 + 10 minutes

STORAGE
Store the cooked burgers for up to 2 days in the refrigerator.

SERVE THIS WITH...
pita bread
Marinated Sardine & Tomato Skewers (see page 66)

OMEGA-3 SOURCES
Canola oil, tuna

NUTRITION FACTS PER PORTION
1.2g. fish omega-3
0.8g. vegetarian omega-3
300 calories
17g. fat
2.5g. saturated fat

2 tbsp. canola oil
14oz. fresh tuna
2 shallots, finely diced
1½ cups breadcrumbs
2 tsp. chili flakes
2 garlic cloves, crushed
2 tbsp. chopped cilantro
2 eggs, beaten
salt
freshly ground black pepper

Relish:
1 large pickled gherkin, finely chopped
1 shallot, finely chopped
2 garlic cloves, finely chopped
½ tbsp. chopped cilantro
2 tbsp. olive oil
2 tbsp. lemon juice

1 Heat half the canola oil in a pan and gently fry the tuna 3 minutes until it is partly cooked.

2 In a bowl, mix the shallots, breadcrumbs, chili, garlic, and cilantro. Season lightly with salt and pepper.

3 Finely chop the tuna and mix it, with the eggs, into the shallot mixture. Cover and set aside in the refrigerator.

4 Mix together all the relish ingredients.

5 Using your hands, shape the tuna mixture into 4 burgers, pressing together firmly. Heat the remaining canola oil in a large pan and brown the burgers 2 to 3 minutes on each side. Serve with a spoonful of the relish.

easy fish pie

Whether served for friends or family, this easy fish pie is ideal for chilly winter evenings.

1lb. 8oz. potatoes, peeled
1/3 cup milk
1 tbsp. olive oil spread
10½oz. salmon fillet
5oz. cod fillet
1 tbsp. olive oil
½ onion, chopped
1 garlic clove, crushed

1¾oz. smoked mackerel fillet, flaked
3½oz. peeled cooked shrimp
½ cup crème fraîche
1oz. cheddar cheese, grated
salt
freshly ground black pepper

1 Preheat the oven to 325°F. Boil the potatoes in a pan of salted water 20 minutes, then mash with the milk and olive oil spread. Season with salt and pepper. Meanwhile, wrap the salmon and cod fillets in foil, set on a baking sheet, and bake 15 minutes. Keep the oven on.
2 Gently heat the oil in a pan, add the onion and garlic, and cook 3 to 4 minutes until softened.
3 Roughly flake the cooked salmon and cod fillets into a large dish. Add the onions, mackerel, shrimp, and crème fraîche. Sprinkle with most of the cheese.
4 Spread the mashed potato over the top and sprinkle with the rest of the cheese. Bake 20 minutes or until the pie is bubbling and brown on top.

SERVES 4

PREPARATION + COOKING
30 + 40 minutes

STORAGE
This can be stored in the refrigerator for up to 3 days or the freezer for up to 3 months.

SERVE THIS WITH...
Cherry Lattice Pie (see page 137)

OMEGA-3 SOURCES
Salmon, cod, mackerel, shrimp

NUTRITION FACTS PER PORTION
1.8g. fish omega-3
420 calories
19g. fat
7g. saturated fat

SERVES 4

PREPARATION + COOKING
10 + 5 minutes

STORAGE
The citrus salsa can be kept in
an airtight container for up to
1 week.

SERVE THIS WITH...
potato salad

OMEGA-3 SOURCES
Mackerel

NUTRITION FACTS PER PORTION
1.8g. fish omega-3
250 calories
18g. fat
3.6g. saturated fat

broiled mackerel fillets with citrus salsa

The citrus salsa is a perfect accompaniment to
the mackerel since it cuts through any oiliness.

2 limes
3 lemons
2 tbsp. chopped pitted black
  olives

2 tbsp. chopped pitted green
  olives
1 large tomato, chopped
1 tbsp. chopped cilantro
4 x 3½oz. mackerel fillets

1 Preheat the broiler and line a broiler pan with foil.
Slice off the zest from the limes and 2 of the lemons,
then chop the fruit, reserving one whole lemon. Put
the chopped fruit in a serving bowl, add the rest of the
chopped ingredients, and mix well.
2 Place the mackerel on the broiler pan and broil for
2–3 minutes on each side.
3 Slice the remaining lemon into wedges and squeeze
them over the fish. Serve with the citrus salsa.

greek mackerel fillets

This dish is inspired by Greek cuisine, with its abundance of fresh fish and olives.

4 x 3½oz. mackerel fillets
2 tbsp. tomato paste
2 garlic cloves, crushed
2 tsp. white wine
8 sun-dried tomatoes, finely
   chopped

¼ cup pitted green olives,
   finely chopped
2 tbsp. capers
1 tbsp. chopped parsley
salt
freshly ground black pepper

1 Preheat the oven to 400°F. Season the mackerel fillets with salt and pepper and place them in a baking dish.
2 Mix together the tomato paste, garlic, and wine to make a paste. Spread the paste over the fillets.
3 Sprinkle the sun-dried tomatoes, olives, and capers over the fish. Cover with foil and bake 30 minutes.
4 Remove the foil, sprinkle with the parsley, and serve.

SERVES 4

PREPARATION + COOKING
10 + 30 minutes

STORAGE
Eat immediately.

SERVE THIS WITH...
pita bread

OMEGA-3 SOURCES
Mackerel

NUTRITION FACTS PER PORTION
1.8 fish omega-3
270 calories
18g. fat
4g. saturated fat

trout with herb crust

Trout has a delicate flavor that pairs well with fresh parsley, cilantro, and basil.

4 x 12oz. trout fillets	1 heaped cup couscous
2 tbsp. canola oil	large handful mixed parsley,
1 large onion, finely chopped	cilantro, and basil, chopped
2 garlic cloves, crushed	1¹/₃ cups Parmesan cheese,
scant 1 cup white wine	grated
2 fish bouillon cubes	freshly ground black pepper

1 Preheat the oven to 375°F. Lay the trout fillets in an ovenproof dish and bake 10 minutes, then set aside, but keep the oven hot.

2 Meanwhile, heat the oil in a pan, add the onion, and cook 5 minutes until softened. Add the garlic and remove from the heat. Add the wine, bouillon, and 1½ cups hot water and stir well. Add the couscous and herbs and let stand a few minutes until the couscous absorbs the liquid.

3 Add half of the Parmesan to the couscous mixture. Season with pepper. Spoon the couscous mixture equally over the fish to form mounds, then sprinkle with the remaining Parmesan. Bake 12 to 15 minutes until the crust is browned. Serve immediately.

baked herring with bacon & tomato

This rich creamy dish is a great way to bake the herring, as it keeps in all the moisture.

1 tbsp. canola oil
1 onion, finely chopped
4 bacon slices, finely chopped
¾ cup mushrooms, chopped
½ zucchini, chopped
4oz. cherry tomatoes, halved
pinch of mixed herbs

3 tbsp. breadcrumbs
2 tbsp. crème fraîche
8 x 2½oz. herring fillets
2 tbsp. olive oil spread
⅓ cup grated Parmesan cheese
salt
freshly ground black pepper

1 Preheat the oven to 375°F. Heat the oil in a pan and fry the onion and bacon 3 minutes. Add the mushrooms, zucchini, and tomatoes and cook 2 minutes. Turn off the heat and mix in the herbs, breadcrumbs, and crème fraîche. Season with salt and pepper.

2 Grease the bottom of a baking dish. Lay 4 herring fillets in the dish, then spoon a thick layer of the mixture on top. Top with the rest of the fillets and press the layers together. Dot with small drops of the olive oil spread, season well, and sprinkle with the Parmesan.

3 Bake 25 minutes until golden, then serve.

SERVES 4

PREPARATION + COOKING
15 + 25 minutes

STORAGE
This is not suitable for the refrigerator or freezer.

SERVE THIS WITH...
green beans
boiled new potatoes

OMEGA-3 SOURCES
Canola oil, herring

NUTRITION FACTS PER PORTION
1.8g. fish omega-3
0.7g. vegetarian omega-3
523 calories
35g. fat
14g. saturated fat

indonesian spicy rice

This is a twist on nasi goreng, the classic Indonesian fried-rice dish.

SERVES 4

PREPARATION + COOKING
10 + 20 minutes

STORAGE
Store in the refrigerator for up to 2 days.

SERVE THIS WITH...
chopped hard-boiled egg

OMEGA-3 SOURCES
Canola oil, shrimp, mackerel

NUTRITION FACTS PER PORTION
0.8g. fish omega-3
1g. vegetarian omega-3
515 calories
19g. fat
2.4g. saturated fat

½ cup long-grain white rice
3 tbsp. canola oil
1 large onion, finely chopped
3 garlic cloves, finely chopped
14oz. cooked, peeled shrimp
2 hot red chilies
3½oz. smoked mackerel fillet, sliced
generous ¹/₃ cup fish stock
2 tbsp. soy sauce
1 tbsp. Thai fish sauce
4 scallions, thinly sliced
8 shrimp crackers

1 Boil the rice 10 to 12 minutes. Drain and set aside. Heat the oil in a pan and fry the onion and garlic 1 minute.
2 Add the shrimp and chilies and stir-fry 1 minute. Add the rice, breaking up any lumps. Stir in the mackerel pieces, stock, soy sauce, and Thai fish sauce. Cook 3 to 4 minutes until the rice is hot throughout.
3 Finally, add the scallions and stir well. Crumble the shrimp crackers on top and serve.

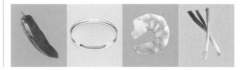

honey-roasted salmon

The delicious natural sweetness of the honey makes this popular with children. It's versatile, too, and tastes great served either hot or cold.

¼ cup (½ stick) butter
¼ cup clear honey
large pinch salt
4 x 5oz. salmon fillets

1 Preheat the oven to 400°F. In a small pan, melt the butter, add the honey and salt, and mix well.

2 Lay the salmon in an baking dish. Pour the honey-butter over the salmon and let marinate 15 minutes.

3 Spoon the honey mixture over the fillets again and bake 20 minutes. Check regularly to ensure that the salmon doesn't burn.

4 Remove from the oven and serve hot.

SERVES 4

PREPARATION + COOKING
20 + 20 minutes

STORAGE
The cooked salmon will keep in the refrigerator for 2 days.

SERVE THIS WITH...
jacket potato
French beans

OMEGA-3 SOURCES
Salmon

NUTRITION FACTS PER PORTION
2.3g. fish omega-3
361 calories
24g. fat
9g. saturated fat

DESSERTS

We all want to enjoy healthier desserts, and sometimes we need a bit of indulgence. Using ingredients such as flax seed, hemp oil, and walnuts, these cleverly adapted recipes boost your omega-3 intake without compromising on taste. Omega-3-rich foods may even help to prevent heart disease; maintain optimum blood pressure and cholesterol levels; and give relief from joint pain, depression, and autoimmune diseases. So why not bite into one of the irresistible Chocolate & Walnut Brownies or dip your spoon into a decadent Lemon Curd Pudding? Who would have known that it would be possible to feel quite so virtuous while enjoying a slice of Chocolate Cheesecake?

Ⓥ Ⓐ Ⓞ Ⓓ Ⓖ Ⓔ Ⓑ Ⓢ

bread pudding

SERVES 6

PREPARATION + COOKING
20 + 40 minutes

STORAGE:
This will keep in the refrigerator
for 3 days or in the freezer for
3 months.

SERVE THIS WITH...
cream or ice cream

OMEGA-3 SOURCES
Canola oil, flax seed, ground flax
seed, walnuts, hemp oil

NUTRITION FACTS PER PORTION
0.7g. vegetarian omega-3
500 calories
26g. fat
8g. saturated fat

This delicious winter dessert freezes well,
ready for days when only comfort food will do.

1 tbsp. canola oil
¼ cup (½ stick) butter, softened
6 slices of Omega Bread
  (see page 72)
1 cup plus 1 tbsp. milk
⅓ cup light cream
1 tbsp. hemp oil
3 eggs, lightly beaten

¼ cup plus 1 tbsp. unrefined
  granulated sugar
1 tsp. vanilla extract
½ tsp. ground cinnamon
⅔ cup raisins
grated zest of ½ lemon
1 tbsp. granulated sugar

1 Preheat the oven to 350°F. Grease a 5-cup baking dish
with the canola oil. Spread the butter generously on one
side of each slice of bread and cut in half diagonally. Put a
layer of bread on the bottom of the dish, buttered-side up.
2 In a bowl, mix together the milk, cream, hemp oil, eggs,
sugar, vanilla, and cinnamon. Pour half the liquid over the
bread, then sprinkle with half the raisins.
3 Place the other slices of bread, overlapping, on top
and pour the rest of the liquid over. Sprinkle with the
remaining raisins, then let soak 10 minutes.
4 Sprinkle with lemon zest and sugar and bake
40 minutes. Serve warm.

hot chocolate pears

A warming autumnal dessert that comes into its own when the evenings start drawing in.

1 tsp. canola oil
2 large pears, peeled, cored and quartered
1 cup self-rising flour
¼ cup ground flax seed
1 tsp. baking powder
¼ cup unsweetened cocoa powder
pinch salt

1 cup sugar
2½oz. semi-sweet chocolate, chopped
2 tbsp. butter, melted
1 egg
1 tbsp. hemp oil
scant 1 cup milk
1 tsp. vanilla extract

1 Preheat the oven to 350°F. Grease a 5-cup baking dish with the canola oil. Put the pears and ½ cup water in a pan and poach gently over medium-low heat 5 minutes. Put the pears in the bottom of the dish.

2 Sift the flour, ground flax seed, baking powder, cocoa, and salt into a bowl. Add the sugar and chocolate.Whisk the remaining ingredients and mix into the dry ingredients. Spoon onto the pears. Bake 35 to 40 minutes, then serve.

SERVES 6

PREPARATION + COOKING
15 + 40 minutes

STORAGE:
Eat within 2 days.

SERVE THIS WITH...
ice cream

OMEGA-3 SOURCES
Canola oil, ground flax seed, hemp oil

NUTRITION FACTS PER PORTION
2g. vegetarian omega-3
440 calories
19g. fat
6.5g. saturated fat

OMEGA-3 SOURCES
Canola oil, ground flax seed, walnuts

NUTRITION FACTS PER PORTION
2.5g. vegetarian omega-3
402 calories
23g. fat
2.8g. saturated fat

apple & peach crumble

Containing vegetarian omega-3 from three different sources, this recipe is a healthier version of the classic crumble. Low in sugar and high in fiber, its omega-3 may help your family's brains stay active and agile. They will happily devour this treat, whether served hot or cold.

1 tbsp. canola oil
1lb. 5oz. cooking apples, such
   as braeburn or gala, peeled,
   cored, and roughly diced
scant 1 cup apple juice
2 tsp. ground cinnamon
2 cloves

½ cup dark brown sugar
2 peaches, pitted and diced
6 tbsp. olive oil spread
1¼ cups all-purpose flour
¼ cup ground flax seed
scant ¾ cup chopped walnuts

SERVES 6

PREPARATION + COOKING
15 + 35 minutes

STORAGE
Store in the refrigerator for 3 days
or freeze for up to 3 months.

SERVE THIS WITH...
whipped cream or ice cream

1 Preheat the oven to 375°F. Grease a large baking dish with the canola oil. Spread the apples over the bottom of the dish and add the apple juice, cinnamon, cloves, and half the sugar.

2 Bake 5 minutes, then add the peaches and return to the oven a further 5 minutes while you make the crumble.

3 In a bowl, lightly rub the olive oil spread into the flour using your fingertips. Mix in the ground flax seed, walnuts, and remaining sugar.

4 Spread the crumble mixture over the fruit and return to the oven 20 to 25 minutes until the crumble is browned and the fruit is soft.

You can use
other fruit to make
this—apricots
and pears work
especially well.

winter rice pudding

SERVES 4

PREPARATION + COOKING
5 minutes + 2 hours

STORAGE:
This can be kept in the refrigerator for 3 days or in the freezer for 3 months.

SERVE THIS WITH...
apricot jam

OMEGA-3 SOURCES
Hemp oil, soy milk

NUTRITION FACTS PER PORTION
3.3g. vegetarian omega-3
415 calories
20g. fat
3g. saturated fat

Traditional baked rice pudding is a great winter warmer. The nuttiness of the hemp oil, combined here with dried fruit, spices, and cloves, is quite delicious. This version is also—amazingly—dairy-free.

¼ cup hemp oil
4¹/₃ cups soy milk
½ tsp. ground nutmeg
½ tsp. ground cinnamon
4 cloves

²/₃ cup arborio rice
½ cup raisins
¹/₃ cup dried apricots, chopped

1 Heat the oven to 300°F. Grease a baking dish with half the hemp oil.

2 In a bowl mix together the soy milk, remaining hemp oil, nutmeg, cinnamon, and cloves.

3 Add the rice and dried fruit to the soy milk mixture and pour into the baking dish.

4 Bake 1½ to 2 hours, depending upon how thick you like your pudding. Set aside 5 minutes before serving.

Ⓥ ⬡ ⬡ ⬡ ⬡ ⬡

chocolate cheesecake

A food processor is essential to make the tofu as smooth as possible in this cheesecake.

¼ cup olive oil spread, melted, plus extra for greasing
scant ½ cup walnuts, toasted
5½oz. chocolate graham crackers

3½oz. semi-sweet chocolate, broken into chunks
9oz. firm tofu
14oz. cream cheese
¼ cup sugar, sifted
1 tbsp. grated dark chocolate

SERVES 10

PREPARATION
25 minutes + chilling

STORAGE
Store in the refrigerator for 3 to 4 days. Not suitable for freezing.

SERVE THIS WITH...
raspberries
strawberries
crème fraîche

OMEGA-3 SOURCES
Walnuts, tofu

NUTRITION FACTS PER PORTION
0.4g. vegetarian omega-3
420 calories
35g. fat
17g. saturated fat

1 Grease an 8in. tart pan with a removable bottom and line it with baking parchment.

2 Finely grind the walnuts and graham crackers in a food processor. Mix in the olive oil spread and then press the mixture into the tart pan, flattening it with a spoon. Chill in the refrigerator while making the filling.

3 Melt the chocolate in a bowl set over a pan of gently simmering water. Meanwhile, blend the tofu and cream cheese in a food processor until smooth, then fold it into the melted chocolate, a little at a time, until completely incorporated and smooth. Stir in the sugar.

4 Pour the mixture over the crust and chill 3 to 4 hours until set. Serve sprinkled with chocolate.

Ⓥ ⚫ ⚫ Ⓞ ⚫ ⚫ ⚫ ⚫

MAKES 16

PREPARATION + COOKING
15 + 25 minutes

STORAGE:
These will keep in an airtight container for up to 1 week or in the freezer for up to 1 month.

SERVE THIS WITH...
ice cream

OMEGA-3 SOURCES
Hemp oil, ground flax seed, walnuts

NUTRITION FACTS PER PORTION
1.6g. vegetarian omega-3
260 calories
16g. fat
6g. saturated fat

chocolate & walnut brownies

These rich, moist brownies are a delicious treat with a feel-good factor.

5½oz. semi-sweet chocolate, broken into chunks
6 tbsp. olive oil spread
⅓ cup hemp oil
3 eggs
heaping ¾ cup unrefined granulated sugar

1½ tsp. vanilla extract
1 cup self-rising flour
¼ cup ground flax seed
½ tsp. salt
½ tsp. baking powder
scant ½ cup chopped walnuts
3oz. white chocolate chips

1 Preheat the oven to 350°F. Melt the chocolate and olive oil spread in a pan over low heat. Stir in the hemp oil, then set aside.

2 Beat together the eggs, sugar, and vanilla extract, then beat in the chocolate mixture. Sift in the flour, ground flax seed, salt, and baking powder. Stir well, then fold in the walnuts and chocolate chips, saving a few chips for the top.

3 Pour the mixture into an 8in. non-stick baking pan, sprinkle with the reserved chocolate chips, and bake 20 to 25 minutes. Remove from the oven and let cool 5 minutes. Cut the brownies into squares while they are warm. Serve warm.

(V) (symbols)

chocolate mousse crunch

Just the name of this gets your mouth watering. A quick dessert for those evenings when time is short but a little treat is required.

3½oz. milk chocolate, broken into chunks
¼ cup canola oil

scant 1 cup Greek yogurt
6 chocolate graham crackers
¼ cup ground flax seed

1 Melt the chocolate in a heatproof bowl set over a pan of simmering water. Whisk the oil into the melted chocolate, then set aside.
2 Fold the yogurt, a little at a time, into the chocolate until completely blended. Spoon into serving bowls.
3 Just before serving, make the topping. Put the chocolate graham crackers in a plastic bag and crush them using a rolling pin. Mix in the flax seed and sprinkle over the chocolate mousses.

SERVES 4

PREPARATION + COOKING
10 + 5 minutes

STORAGE:
This can be chilled in the refrigerator, without the topping, for up to 3 days.

SERVE THIS WITH...
orange segments

OMEGA-3 SOURCES
Canola oil, ground flax seed

NUTRITION FACTS PER PORTION
1.3g. vegetarian omega-3
210 calories
12g. fat
1.9g. saturated fat

lemon curd puddings

OMEGA-3 SOURCES
Canola oil, ground flax seed

NUTRITION FACTS PER PORTION
2.2g. vegetarian omega-3
360 calories
17g. fat
2.6g. saturated fat

Ground flax seed lends these delightful little puddings a slightly nutty flavor. Small but powerful, these slim seeds not only contain useful omega-3 fats but are also a good source of fiber. They need to be ground down to release their full potential, however, as this allows their turbo-charged nutrients to be absorbed by your body.

1 tbsp. canola oil
juice and zest of 1 lemon
4 tbsp. lemon curd
¼ cup olive oil spread
¼ cup plus 1 tbsp. unrefined
   granulated sugar

1 egg, beaten
1 cup self-rising flour
1 tsp. baking powder
¼ cup ground flax seed

SERVES 4

PREPARATION + COOKING
15 + 25 minutes

STORAGE
Store in an airtight container for
up to 3 days.

SERVE THIS WITH...
vanilla ice cream
custard sauce

1 Preheat the oven to 350°F. Grease four individual
ramekins with the canola oil and place them in a roasting
pan. Mix the lemon juice into the lemon curd, then put
1 tablespoon of the mixture into each ramekin.
2 In a large bowl, cream together the olive oil spread
and sugar. Add the egg and sift in the flour and baking
powder. Add the flax seed and gently fold it all together.
Stir in the lemon zest and about 2 tablespoons hot water
to make a pourable consistency.
3 Divide the mixture into the ramekins. Pour boiling water
into the roasting pan until it reaches halfway up the sides
of the ramekins. Make a loose "tent" of foil over the top of
the roasting pan and bake 25 minutes.
4 Let them stand 5 minutes, then turn out and serve.

> For a winter
> variation, add
> some chopped
> candied ginger to
> the lemon curd
> sauce.

Ⓥ ⚫ Ⓞ ⚫ ⚫ ⚫ ⚫

carrot gateau

Fresh carrots, blueberries, and strawberries make this an antioxidant-packed dessert.

SERVES 10

PREPARATION + COOKING
15 + 35 minutes

STORAGE:
The undecorated cake will keep in an airtight container for 1 week. Once decorated, eat within 3 days.

SERVE THIS WITH...
strawberries
blueberries

OMEGA-3 SOURCES
Canola oil, flax seed oil, ground flax seed

NUTRITION FACTS PER PORTION
4g. vegetarian omega-3
370 calories
18g. fat
4g. saturated fat

¹/₃ cup canola oil
3 tbsp. flax seed oil
scant 1 cup brown sugar
2 eggs, beaten
1¼ cups self-rising flour
½ cup ground flax seed
1 heaping cup grated carrot
1½ cups golden raisins
3 tsp. pumpkin pie spice

1½ tsp. baking soda
juice and zest of 1 orange

Topping:
3½oz. cream cheese
½ cup powdered sugar
2 tsp. lemon juice
½ cup blueberries
½ cup strawberries

1 Preheat the oven to 325°F. Grease an 8in. cake pan with 1 teaspoon of the canola oil. Line it with baking parchment.
2 Whisk together the oils, sugar, and eggs. Fold in all the other ingredients, except the juice, and pour into the pan. Bake 35 minutes. Pour the juice over the cake and let cool.
3 Combine the cream cheese, powdered sugar, and lemon juice, spread it over the cake, and pile the fruit on top.

Ⓥ ⓢ ⓓ ⓦ ⓢ ⓔ

cherry lattice pie

This light pastry dough is very crumbly, so handle it carefully when assembling the pie.

2¼ cups all-purpose flour
⅓ cup ground flax seed
½ cup (1 stick) plus 1 tbsp.
   butter
⅓ cup sugar

4½ tsp. hemp oil
1lb. 12oz. canned cherries in
   syrup
1 tbsp. cornstarch
1 tbsp. milk

1 Preheat the oven to 350°F. Sift the flour and flax seed into a bowl, adding in the bran left behind. Rub in the butter until the mixture resembles breadcrumbs. Stir in the sugar, then the oil and 2 tablespoons cold water to bind the dough. Wrap in plastic wrap and chill.

2 Drain the syrup from the cherries into a pan. In a small bowl, mix 1 tablespoon of the syrup with the cornstarch. Heat the remaining syrup until it bubbles. Remove from the heat, stir in the cornstarch mixture, and heat a few seconds until thick.

3 Roll out the dough to ¼in. thick and line an 8in. pie plate. Trim and set aside the excess dough. Bake the crust 15 minutes. Cut the remaining dough into thin strips.

4 Fill the pie shell with the cherries and pour in the syrup. Lay the dough strips in a lattice across the pie, brush with the milk, and bake 15 minutes until golden.

SERVES 8

PREPARATION + COOKING
30 + 35 minutes

STORAGE:
This will keep in the refrigerator for 4 days.

SERVE THIS WITH...
vanilla ice cream or crème fraîche

OMEGA-3 SOURCES
Ground flax seed, hemp oil

NUTRITION FACTS PER PORTION
2.1g. vegetarian omega-3
370 calories
15g. fat
6g. saturated fat

Ⓥ ⦿ Ⓞ ⦿ ⦿ ⦿ ⦿ ⦿

baked apple streusel cake

This light and fruity dessert packs an omega-3 punch thanks to its spiced nut topping.

SERVES 8

PREPARATION + COOKING
15 + 40 minutes

STORAGE:
This cake will keep in the refrigerator for up to a week.

SERVE THIS WITH...
crème fraîche

OMEGA-3 SOURCES
Canola oil, flax seed oil, ground flax seed, walnuts

NUTRITION FACTS PER PORTION
6g. vegetarian omega-3
420 calories
22g. fat
2.2g. saturated fat

1½ tsp. canola oil
⅓ cup flax seed oil
⅔ cup unrefined granulated
   sugar
1 egg, beaten
1 cup self-rising flour
½ tsp. baking powder
¼ cup ground flax seed
pinch of salt
2 tbsp. milk

2 large apples, such as
   braeburn or gala, peeled
   and cored

Streusel Topping:
2 tbsp. olive oil spread
¼ cup wholewheat flour
½ cup brown sugar
1 cup chopped walnuts
1 tsp. ground cinnamon

1 Preheat the oven to 350°F. Mix together all of the cake ingredients, except the apples. Beat until smooth, adding more milk if needed to make a dropping consistency. Spoon evenly into a 8in. non-stick springform pan.

2 Grate the apples over the mixture. To make the topping, rub the olive oil spread into the flour until the mixture resembles fine breadcrumbs. Add the sugar, walnuts, and cinnamon and sprinkle over the apple.

3 Bake 35 minutes. Let cool 5 minutes, then serve.

Ⓥ ⓐ ⓕ ⓐ ⓕ ⓐ

baklava

A tiny slice of this decadent nut pastry from
the eastern Mediterranean packs a real punch.

½ cup canola oil
9oz. phyllo dough
scant 1 cup chopped walnuts
¾ cup roughly chopped
   pistachio nuts
¼ cup ground flax seed
1 tsp. ground cinnamon

Syrup:
heaping ⅔ cup sugar
1tbsp. lemon juice
1 tbsp. clear honey

1 Preheat the oven to 350°F. Use 2 teaspoons of the
canola oil to grease the bottom and sides of a 9x12in.
baking pan.
2 Unroll the phyllo dough and trim the sheets to fit the
pan. Brush half the sheets of dough with a little oil, layer
them into the pan, and sprinkle evenly with the nuts,
ground flax seed, and cinnamon. Brush and layer the
remaining sheets of dough, including the top layer.
3 Cut into 24 squares. Bake 20 minutes until golden.
Remove from the oven and let cool.
4 Simmer the sugar, lemon juice, and ⅔ cup water in a
pan 15 minutes, stirring occasionally. Add the honey and
pour the mixture over the baklava. Let the baklava absorb
the syrup, ideally overnight, before serving.

SERVES 6

PREPARATION + COOKING
30 + 15 minutes
+ soaking

STORAGE:
This will keep in the refrigerator
for up to 2 weeks. It can be
frozen for 1 month.

SERVE THIS WITH…
Greek yogurt
crème fraîche
apricots

OMEGA-3 SOURCES
Canola oil, walnuts,
ground flax seed

NUTRITION FACTS PER PORTION
1.4g. vegetarian omega-3
320 calories
21g. fat
1.8g. saturated fat

menu plans

nut-free 5-day menu

An allergy to nuts is an increasingly reported problem. These recipes exclude all nuts, including coconut and pine nuts, but include seeds. Choose from the following daily suggestions, remembering to pepper them with recipes from your regular low-fat diet.

Day 1
Breakfast: Tuna & Bacon Hash Browns (page 35)
Lunch: Shrimp & Chorizo Tapas (page 57)
Dinner: Parmesan Peppers with Balsamic Tofu (page 91)

Day 2
Breakfast: Fruity Maple Oatmeal (page 25)
Lunch: Smoked Mackerel Dip (page 60)
Dinner: Thai Soybean Cakes with Red Pepper Sauce (page 93)

Day 3
Breakfast: Smoked Trout & Poached Egg on Toast (page 34)
Lunch: Dolcelatte Tart (page 50)
Dinner: Spicy Crab Linguine (page 98)

Day 4
Breakfast: Mango & Banana Smoothie (page 24)
Lunch: Five-Spice Tofu Salad (page 44)
Dinner: Seafood Phyllo Tarts (page 62)

Day 5
Breakfast: American Pancakes (page 26)
Lunch: Hummus (page 54)
Dinner: Honey-Roasted Salmon (page 123)

gluten- & wheat-free 5-day menu

If you're intolerant to wheat and gluten it can be difficult to find recipes. Additionally, these recipes are wheat-, rye-, barley- and oat-free. You don't need to eat omega-3 at every meal to get your daily intake, but here are some ideas to ring the changes at breakfast, lunch and dinner.

Day 1
Breakfast: Tuna & Bacon Hash Browns (page 35)
Lunch: Three-Bean Tuscan Soup (page 38)
Dinner: Seafood Paella (page 97)

Day 2
Breakfast: Kedgeree (page 31)
Lunch: Tofu Mushrooms with Gruyère Crust (page 52)
Dinner: Moules Marinière (page 96)

Day 3
Breakfast: Smoked Salmon Omelet (page 32)

Lunch: Smoked Salmon Tarts (page 64)
Dinner: Seafood & Lentil Stew (page 104)

Day 4
Breakfast: Kedgeree (page 31)
Lunch: Curried Hemp & Nut Roast (page 88)
Dinner: Thai Shrimp Curry (page 105)

Day 5
Breakfast: Mango & Banana Smoothie (page 24)
Lunch: Watercress, Walnut, Pear & Roquefort Salad (page 42)
Dinner: Greek Mackerel Fillets (page 119)

vegetarian 5-day menu

Tofu, soybeans, flax seed, and walnuts are good sources of vegetarian omega-3. These recipes help you to overcome the challenge of including omega-3 fats without making your diet too high in calories. You can pick and choose from these meal suggestions across five days.

Day 1
Breakfast: Oaty Breakfast Bar (page 23)
Lunch: Soy & Hemp Falafels (page 53)
Dinner: Bean & Vegetable Chili (page 90)

Day 2
Breakfast: American Pancakes (page 26)
Lunch: Japanese Tofu Stir-fry
    (page 89)
Dinner: Thai Soybean Cakes with Red
    Pepper Sauce (page 93)

Day 3
Breakfast: Fruity Maple Oatmeal (page 25)
Lunch: Soybean & Tofu Laksa (page 92)
Dinner: Curried Hemp & Nut Roast
    (page 88)

Day 4
Breakfast: Breakfast Granola (page 22)
Lunch: Dressed Green Salad (page 43)
    with a slice of Omega Bread
    (page 72)
Dinner: Moroccan Tagine (page 94)

Day 5
Breakfast: Scrambled Tofu on Toast
    (page 30)
Lunch: Three-Bean Tuscan Soup (page 38)
    with a slice of Omega Bread
    (page 72)
Dinner: Walnut & Arugula Pesto Pasta
    (page 51)

children's 5-day menu

Omega-3 fats may help childrens' brain development and concentration. What better way to employ those active minds and hands than by letting them help cook these child-friendly recipes? Here are ideas for breakfast, lunch and dinner—to mix in with your kids' normal diet.

Day 1
Breakfast: American Pancakes (page 26)
Lunch: Hummus with crudités (page 54)
Dinner: Tuna in Tomato Sauce (page 114)

Day 2
Breakfast: French Toast (page 28)
Lunch: Soy & Hemp Falafels (page 53)
Dinner: Salmon & Spinach Risotto
(page 107)

Day 3
Breakfast: Mango & Banana Smoothie
(page 24)
Lunch: Smoked Mackerel Dip sandwiches
(page 60) followed by a Hemp & Honey
Cookie (page 78)
Dinner: Pissaladière (page 115)

Day 4
Breakfast: Small portion of Mango &
Banana Smoothie (page 24) and
Oaty Breakfast Bar (page 23)
Lunch: Spicy Tuna Burgers (page 116)
Dinner: Walnut & Arugula Pesto Pasta
(page 51)

Day 5
Breakfast: Breakfast Granola (page 22)
Lunch: Seeded Flatbread (page 70) served
with Three-Bean Tuscan Soup (page 38)
Dinner: Easy Fish Pie (page 117)

INDEX

31901050614140

BSITES:
canheart.org
andstroke.ca
www.nih.gov